# 3rd Workshop on Hybrid Approaches to Translation

# (HyTra 2014)

**Held at the 14th Conference of the European Chapter of the Association for Computational Linguistics**

## Gothenburg, Sweden
## 27 April 2014

ISBN: 978-1-63266-405-1

**Printed from e-media with permission by:**

Curran Associates, Inc.
57 Morehouse Lane
Red Hook, NY 12571



Printed by Curran Associates, Inc. (2014)

For permission requests, please contact the Association for Computational Linguistics at the address below.

Association for Computational Linguistics
209 N. Eighth Street
Stroudsburg, Pennsylvania 18360

Phone: 1-570-476-8006
Fax: 1-570-476-0860

acl@aclweb.org

**Additional copies of this publication are available from:**

Curran Associates, Inc.
57 Morehouse Lane
Red Hook, NY 12571 USA
Phone: 845-758-0400
Fax: 845-758-2634
Email: curran@proceedings.com
Web: www.proceedings.com

# Introduction

The Third Workshop on Hybrid Approaches to Translation (HyTra) intends to further progress on the findings from the second HyTra, held at ACL 2013, and first HyTra which was held (together with the ESIRMT workshop) as a joint 2-day EACL 2012 workshop. The first editions of HyTra brought together researchers working on diverse aspects of hybrid machine translation. HyTra proceedings put together high-quality papers experimenting with current topics including statistical approaches integrating morphological, syntactic, semantic and rule-based information.

Machine Translation (MT) is a highly interdisciplinary and multidisciplinary field since it is approached from the point of view of human translators, engineers, computer scientists, mathematicians and linguists. This workshop aims at motivating the cooperation and interaction between them, and to foster innovative combinations between the two main MT paradigms: statistical and rule-based.

The advantages of statistical MT are fast development cycles, low cost, robustness, superior lexical selection and relative fluency due to the use of language models. But (pure) statistical MT has also disadvantages: It needs large amounts of data, which for many language pairs are not available, and are unlikely to become available in the foreseeable future. This problem is especially relevant for under-resourced languages. Recent advances in factored morphological models and syntax-based models in SMT indicate that non-statistical symbolic representations and processing models need to have their proper place in MT research and development, and more research is needed to understand how to develop and integrate these non-statistical models most efficiently.

The advantages of rule-based MT are that its rules and representations are geared towards human understanding and can be more easily checked, corrected and exploited for applications outside of machine translation such as dictionaries, text understanding and dialog systems. But (pure) rule-based MT has also severe disadvantages, among them slow development cycles, high cost, a lack of robustness in the case of incorrect input, and difficulties in making correct choices with respect to ambiguous words, structures, and transfer equivalents.

The translations of statistical systems are often surprisingly good with respect to phrases and short distance collocations, but they often fail when selectional preferences need to be based on more distant words. In contrast, the output of rule-based systems is often surprisingly good if the parser assigns the correct analysis to a sentence. However, it usually leaves something to be desired if the correct analysis cannot be computed, or if there is not enough information for selecting the correct target words when translating ambiguous words and structures. Given the complementarity of statistical and rule-based MT, it is natural that the boundaries among them have narrowed. The question is what the combined architecture should look like. In the past few years, in the MT scientific community, the interest in hybridization and system combination has significantly increased. This is why a large number of approaches for constructing hybrid MT have already been proposed offering a considerable potential of improving MT quality and efficiency. There is also great potential in expanding hybrid MT systems with techniques, tools and processing resources from other areas of NLP, such as Information Extraction, Information Retrieval, Question Answering, Semantic Web, Automatic Semantic Inferencing. The aim of the proposed workshop is to bring together and share ideas among researchers developing statistical, example-based, or rule-based translation systems and who enhance MT systems with elements from the other approaches. Hereby a focus will be on effectively combining linguistic and data driven approaches (rule-based and statistical MT).

**Organizers:**

Rafael E. Banchs (Institute for Infocomm Research, Singapore)
Marta R. Costa-jussà (Institute for Infocomm Research, Singapore)
Reinhard Rapp (Universities of Aix-Marseille and Mainz)
Patrik Lambert (Pompeu Fabra University, Barcelona)
Kurt Eberle (Lingenio GmbH, Heidelberg)
Bogdan Babych (University of Leeds)

**Invited Speakers:**

Hans Uszkoreit (Saarland University and DFKI, Germany) Abstract.
Joakim Nivre (Uppsala University, Sweden)

**Program Committee:**

Ahmet Aker, University of Sheffield, UK
Bogdan Babych, University of Leeds, UK
Rafael E. Banchs, Institute for Infocomm Research, Singapore
Alexey Baytin, Yandex, Moscow, Russia
Núria Bel, Universitat Pompeu Fabra, Barcelona, Spain
Pierrette Bouillon, ISSCO/TIM/ETI, University of Geneva, Switzerland
Michael Carl, Copenhagen Business School, Denmark
Marta R. Costa-jussa, Institute for Infocomm Research, Singapore
Oliver Culo, University of Mainz, Germany
Kurt Eberle, Lingenio GmbH, Heidelberg, Germany
Andreas Eisele, DGT (European Commission), Luxembourg
Marcello Federico, Fondazione Bruno Kessler, Trento, Italy
Christian Federmann, Language Technology Lab, DFKI, Saarbrücken, Germany
José A. R. Fonollosa, Universitat Politècnica de Catalunya, Barcelona, Spain
Maxim Khalilov, TAUS, Amsterdam, The Netherlands
Patrik Lambert, Pompeu Fabra University, Barcelona, Spain
Udo Kruschwitz, University of Essex, UK
Yanjun Ma, Baidu Inc., Beijing, China
José B. Mariño, Universitat Politècnica de Catalunya, Barcelona, Spain
Bart Mellebeek, University of Amsterdam, The Netherlands
Hermann Ney, RWTH Aachen, Germany
Reinhard Rapp, Universities of Aix-Marseille, France, and Mainz, Germany
Anders Søgaard, University of Copenhagen, Denmark
Wade Shen, Massachusetts Institute of Technology, Cambridge, USA
Serge Sharoff, University of Leeds, UK
George Tambouratzis, Institute for Language and Speech Processing, Athens, Greece
Jörg Tiedemann, University of Uppsala, Sweden

# Table of Contents

# Workshop Program

**09:00-10:30** **Session 1**

09:00-09:45 Invited Talk: *Analytical Approaches to Combining MT Technologies*
Hans Uszkoreit

09:45-10:00 *Using Hypothesis Selection Based Features for Confusion Network MT System Combination*
Sahar Ghannay and Loïc Barrault

10:00-10:15 *Comparing CRF and template-matching in phrasing tasks within a Hybrid MT system*
George Tambouratzis

10:15-10:30 *Controlled Authoring In A Hybrid Russian-English Machine Translation System*
Svetlana Sheremetyeva

**10:30-11:00** **Coffee Break**

**11:00-12:45** **Session 2**

11:00-11:15 *Using Feature Structures to Improve Verb Translation in English-to-German Statistical MT*
Philip Williams and Philipp Koehn

11:15-11:30 *Building a Spanish-German Dictionary for Hybrid MT*
Anne Göhring

11:30-11:45 *An Empirical Study of the Impact of Idioms on Phrase Based Statistical Machine Translation of English to Brazilian-Portuguese*
Giancarlo Salton, Robert Ross and John Kelleher

11:45-12:00 *Resumptive Pronoun Detection for Modern Standard Arabic to English MT*
Stephen Tratz, Clare Voss and Jamal Laoudi

12:00-12:15 *Automatic Building and Using Parallel Resources for SMT from Comparable Corpora*
Santanu Pal, Partha Pakray and Sudip Kumar Naskar

12:15-12:30 *Improving the precision of automatically constructed human-oriented translation dictionaries*
Alexandra Antonova and Alexey Misyurev

**12:45-14:00** **Lunch Break**

**14:00-14:45** **Session 3**

14:00-14:45 Invited Talk: *Adventures in Multilingual Parsing*
Joakim Nivre

**15:00-15:30** **Industry Session: Added value of hybrid methods in Machine Translation from a commercial perspective - Part 1**

15:00-15:30 Maxim Khalilov, bmmt GmbH
*Machine translation for LSPs: strategy and implementation*

**15:30-16:00** **Coffee Break with Poster Session**

*A Principled Approach to Context-Aware Machine Translation*
Rafael E. Banchs

*Deriving de/het gender classification for Dutch nouns for rule-based MT generation tasks*
Bogdan Babych, Jonathan Geiger, Mireia Ginestí Rosell and Kurt Eberle

*Chinese-to-Spanish rule-based machine translation system*
Jordi Centelles and Marta R. Costa-jussà

*Extracting Multiword Translations from Aligned Comparable Documents*
Reinhard Rapp and Serge Sharoff

**16:00-18:00** **Industry Session: Added value of hybrid methods in Machine Translation from a commercial perspective - Part 2**

16:00-16:30 Adrià de Gispert, SDL Research
*SDL Research: bringing research in MT from the lab to the product*

16:30-17:00 Josep M. Crego, SYSTRAN
*tba*

17:00-17:30 Andrejy Vasiljevs, Tilde
*How to overtake Google in MT quality - the Baltic case*

17:30-18:00 Kurt Eberle, Lingenio GmbH
*Hybrid Strategies for better products and shorter time-to-market*

**18:00-18:15** **Concluding Remarks and Discussion**

# Analytical Approaches to Combining MT Technologies

**Hans Uszkoreit**

Dept. of Computational Linguistics
and Phonetics
Saarland University Saarbrücken
&
German Research Center for Artificial
Intelligence (DFKI)
DFKI Language Technology Lab
Germany
Hans.Uszkoreit@dfki.de

## Abstract

The talk will report on recent and ongoing work dedicated to analytical methods for a systematic combination of observed strengths of translation technologies. The focus will be on different ways of exploiting existing data on MT output and performance measures for system combination and for gaining insights on strengths and weaknesses of existing technologies.

# Using Hypothesis Selection Based Features for Confusion Network MT System Combination

**Sahar Ghannay**
LIUM, University of Le Mans
Le Mans, France
Sahar.Gannay.Etu@univ-lemans.fr

**Loïc Barrault**
LIUM, University of Le Mans
Le Mans, France
loic.barrault@lium.univ-lemans.fr

## Abstract

This paper describes the development operated into MANY, an open source system combination software based on confusion networks developed at LIUM. The hypotheses from Chinese-English MT systems were combined with a new version of the software. MANY has been updated in order to use word confidence score and to boost $n$-grams occurring in input hypotheses. In this paper we propose either to use an adapted language model or adding some additional features in the decoder to boost certain $n$-grams probabilities. Experimental results show that the updates yielded significant improvements in terms of BLEU score.

## 1 Introduction

MANY (Barrault, 2010) is an open source system combination software based on Confusion Networks (CN). The combination by confusion networks generates an exponential number of hypotheses. Most of these hypotheses contain $n$-grams do not exist in input hypotheses. Some of these new $n$-grams are ungrammatical, despite the presence of a language model. These novel $n$-grams are due to errors in hypothesis alignment and the confusion network structure. In section 3 we present two methods used to boost $n$-grams present in input hypotheses.

Currently, decisions taken by the decoder mainly depend on the language model score, which is deemed insufficient to precisely evaluate the hypotheses. In consequence, it is interesting to estimate a score for better judging their quality. The challenge of our work is to exploit certain parameters defined by (Almut Siljaand and Vogel, 2008) to calculate word confidence score. These features are detailed in section 4. The approach is evaluated on the internal data of the BOLT project. Some experiments have been performed on the Chinese-English system combination task. The experimental results are presented in section 5. Before that, a quick description of MANY, including recent developments can be found in section 2.

## 2 System description

MANY is a system combination software (Barrault, 2010) based on the decoding of a lattice made of several Confusion Networks (CN). This is a widespread approach in MT system combination, see *e.g.* (Antti-Veikko I.Rosti and Schwartz, 2007; Damianos Karakos and Dreyer, 2008; Shen et al., 2008; Antti-Veikko I. Rosti and Schw, 2009). MANY can be decomposed in two main modules. The first one is the alignment module which is a modified version of TERp (Matthew G. Snover and Schwartz, 2009). Its role is to incrementally align the hypotheses against a backbone in order to create a confusion network. 1-best hypotheses from all $M$ systems are aligned in order to build $M$ confusion networks (one for each system considered as backbone). These confusion networks are then connected together to create a lattice. This module uses different costs (which corresponds to a match, an insertion, a deletion, a substitution, a shift, a synonym and a stem) to compute the best alignment and incrementally build a confusion network. In the case of confusion network, the match (substitution, synonym, and stem) costs are considered when the word in the hypothesis matches (is a substitution, a synonym or a stem of) at least one word of the considered confusion sets in the CN. The second module is the decoder. This decoder is based on the token pass algorithm and it accepts as input the lattice previously created. The probabilities computed in the decoder can be expressed as follow :

$$\log(P_w) = \sum_i \alpha_i \log(h_i(t)) \qquad (1)$$

where $t$ is the hypothesis, the $\alpha_i$ are the weights of the feature functions $h_i$ .

The following features are considered for decoding:

- The language model probability: the probability given by a 4-gram language model.
- The word penalty: penalty depending on the size (in words) of the hypothesis.
- The null-arc penalty: penalty depending on the number of null-arcs crossed in the lattice to obtain the hypothesis.
- System weights: each system receives a weight according to its importance. Each word receives a weight corresponding to the sum of the weights of all systems which proposed it.

Our goal is to include the following ones:

- Word confidence score: each word is given a score, which is the combination of the three scores described in section 4 (equation 7).
- $n$-gram count: number of $n$-grams present in input hypotheses for each combined hypothesis.

In most cases, the new features have best weights according to MERT (*e.g.* the best decoding weights of these features by combining two systems are: lm-weight: 0.049703, word-penalty: 0.0605602, null-penalty: 0.319905, **weight-word-score: -0.378226**, **weight-ngram-count: -0.11687**, priors: 0.0141794#-0.0605561).

## 3 boost $n$-grams

We defined two methods to boost $n$-grams present in input hypotheses. The first one is adding the count of $bi$ or $tri$-grams like a new feature to the decoder as mentioned in Section 2. The second method is using an adapted language model (LM) to decode the lattice, in order to modify $n$-grams probabilities, that have been observed in input hypotheses.

### Language models

Three 4-gram language models named *LM-Web*, *LM-Tune* and *LM-Test*, are used to interpolate the adapted LM. They were trained respectively on the English web Corpus and the system outputs : development and test sets (except their references) involved in system combination, using the SRILM Toolkit (Stolcke, 2002). The resulting model from the interpolation of *LM-Tune* and *LM-Test* is interpolated linearly with the *LM-Web* to build the adapted LM. These models are tuned to minimize the perplexity on the tune reference.

## 4 Word confidence score

The best hypothesis selection relies on several features. In (Barrault, 2011) decisions taken by the decoder depend mainly on a $n$-gram language model, but it is sometimes insufficient to evaluate correctly the quality of the hypotheses. In order to improve these decisions, some additional information should be used. Several researches presented some studies of confidence scores at word and sentence level, such as (Almut Siljaand and Vogel, 2008) and (Ueffing and Ney, 2007). A large set of confidence scores were calculated over the $n$-best list. (Almut Siljaand and Vogel, 2008) defines several features extracted from $n$-best lists (at the sentence level) to select the best hypothesis in a combination approach via hypothesis selection. The challenge of our work is to exploit these features to estimate a confidence score at the word level and injecting it into the confusion networks. The following features are considered:

### Word agreement score based on a window of size *t* around position *i*

This score represents the relative frequency of hypotheses in the $n$-best lists containing the word ***e*** in a window of size *t* around the position *i*. It is computed as follows:

$$\mathrm{WA}_k(e_{i,t}) = \frac{1}{N_k}\sum_{p=0}^{N_k} f(e_{p,i-t}^{p,i+t}, e) \qquad (2)$$

where $N_K$ is the number of hypotheses in the n-best list for the corresponding source sentence $k$, t={0, 1 or 2} and $f(S_i^j, w)$ =1 if $w$ appears in the word sequence $S_i^j$.

When $t$ equals 0, this means that $i = t$, then this score only depends on words at the exact position $i$. The agreement score is calculated accordingly:

$$\text{WA}_k(e_i) = \frac{1}{N_k} \sum_{p=0}^{N_k} f(e_{p,i}, e) \quad (3)$$

The two equations described above, are handled in our contribution, thus the final word agreement score is the average between them if $\text{WA}_k(e_i) \neq 0$ otherwise it is equal to $\text{WA}_k(e_{i,t})$ score.

### Position independent $n$-best List $n$-gram Agreement

This score represents the percentage of hypotheses in the $n$-best lists that contain the $n$-gram $e^i_{i-(n-1)}$, independently of its position in the sentence, as shown in Equation 4. For each hypothesis the $n$-gram is counted only once.

$$\text{NA}_k(e^i_{i-(n-1)}) = \frac{1}{N_k} \sum_{p=0}^{N_k} f(e^i_{i-(n-1)}, e^I_{1,p}) \quad (4)$$

where $f(e^i_{i-(n-1)}, e^I_{1,p}) = 1$ if the $n$-gram $e^i_{i-(n-1)}$ exists in the $p^{th}$ hypothesis of the $n$-best list. We use $n$-gram lengths of 2 and 3 as two separate features.
The position independent $n$-best list word agreement is the average count of $n$-grams that contain the word $e$. It is computed as:

$$\text{NA}_k(e_i) = \frac{1}{N_{ng}} \sum_{n=0}^{N_{ng}} \text{NA}_k(e^i_{i-(n-1)}) \quad (5)$$

Were $N_{ng}$ is the number of $n$-grams of hypothesis $k$.

### N-best list $n$-gram probability

This score is a traditional $n$-gram language model probability. The $n$-gram probability for a target word $e_i$ given its history $e^{i-1}_{i-(n-1)}$ is defined as:

$$\text{NP}_k(e_i | e^{i-1}_{i-(n-1)}) = \frac{C(e^i_{i-(n-1)})}{C(e^{i-1}_{i-(n-1)})} \quad (6)$$

Where $C(e^i_{i-(n-1)})$ is the count of the $n$-gram $e^i_{i-(n-1)}$ in the $n$-best list for the hypothesis $k$.
The $n$-best list word probability $\text{NP}_k(e_i)$ is the average of the $n$-grams probabilities that contain the word $e$.
The word confidence score is computed using these three features as follows:

$$S_k(e_i) = \frac{\text{WA}_k(e_i) + \sum_{j \in NG} \text{NA}_k(e_i)^j + \text{NP}_k(e_i)^j}{1 + 2 * |NG|} \quad (7)$$

where $NG$ is the set of $n$-gram order, experimentally defined as NG={2-gram, 3-gram} and t = 2. Each $n$-gram order in the set $NG$ is considered as a separate feature.

## 5 Experiments

During experiments, data from the BOLT project on the Chinese to English translation task are used. The outputs (200-best lists) of eight translation systems were provided by the partners. The best six systems were used for combination. *Syscomtune* is used as development set and *Dev* as internal test, these corpora are described in Table 1:

| NAME | #sent. | #words. |
|---|---|---|
| Syscomtune | 985 | 28671 |
| Dev | 1124 | 26350 |

Table 1: BOLT corpora : number of sentences and words calculated on the reference.

To explore the impact of each new feature on the results, they are tested one by one (added one by one in the decoder) then both, given that, the oldest ones are used in all cases. These tests are named respectively **boost-ngram**, **CS-ngram** and **Boost-ngram+CS-ngram** later.

The language model is used to guide the decoding in order to improve translation quality, therefore we evaluated the baseline combination system and each test (described above) with two LMs named *LM-Web* and *LM-ad* and compared their performance in terms of BLEU. By comparing their perplexities, that are respectively *295.43* and *169.923*, we observe a relative reduction of about *42.5%*, that results in an improvement of BLEU score.

Figure 1 shows the results of combining the best systems (up to 6) using these models, that achieved respectively an improvement of *0.85* and *1.17* %BLEU point relatively to the best single system. In the remaining experiments we assume that *MANY-LM-Web* is the baseline.

Figure 2 shows interesting differences in how approaches to boost n-gram estimates behave when the number of input systems is varied. This is due to the fact that results are conditioned by the number and quality of $n$-grams added to the lattice

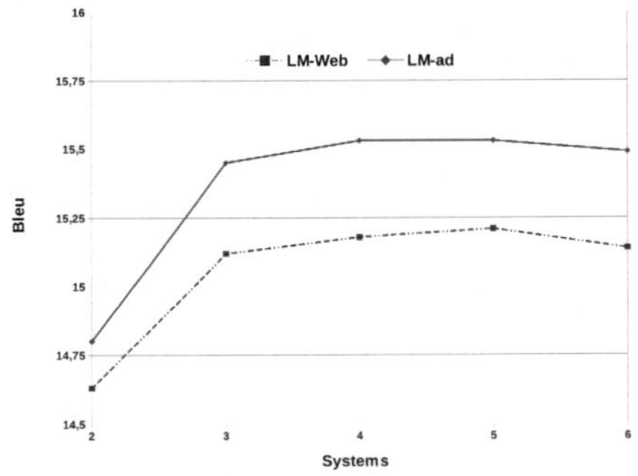


Figure 1: Performance (%BLEU-cased) of MANY after reassessment by LM-Web and LM-ad on the test set.

when the number of systems is varied, that provides varied outputs. In consequence, we observe that using the adapted LM is better than $n$-gram count feature to boost $n$-grams, indeed it guarantees $n$-grams quality.

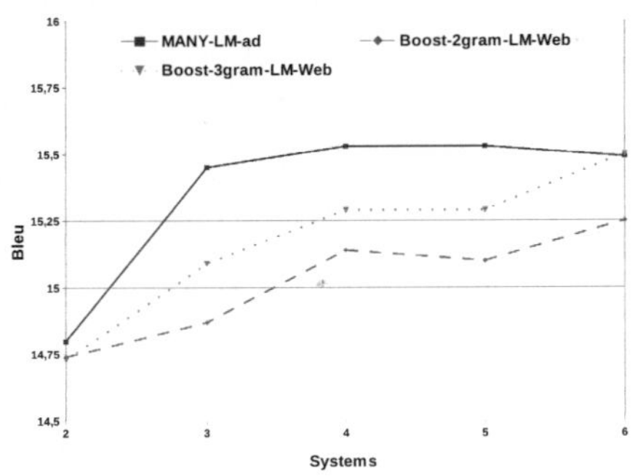


Figure 2: Comparison of $n$-gram boost approaches.

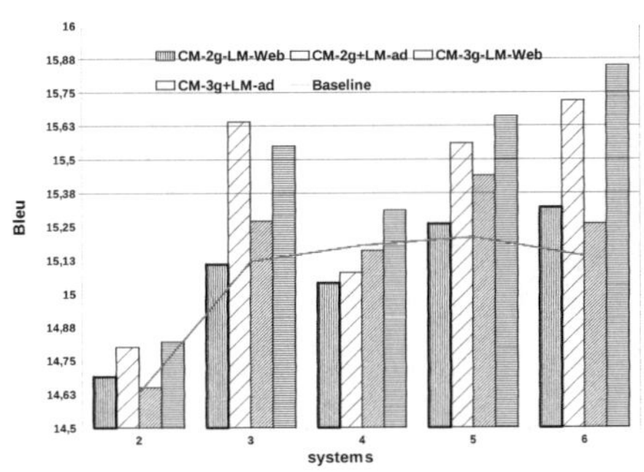


Figure 3: The impact of confidence score on the results when using LM-Web and LM-ad for decoding.

The 200-best lists are operated to estimate the word confidence score that contributes the most to the improvement of results when several (up to 6) systems are combined, as described in Figure 3, whatever the language model used, compared to the baseline. In addition, it seems that the confidence score performs better with the adapted LM than *LM-Web*.

| Systems | BLEU |
|---|---|
| Best single | **14.36** |
| Sys2 | 14.21 |
| Sys3 | 13.76 |
| Sys4 | 13.52 |
| Sys5 | 13.36 |
| Sys6 | 12.99 |
| *MANY+LM-Web(baseline)* | **15.14** |
| Boost-2gram+LM-Web | 15.25 |
| Boost-3gram+LM-Web | 15.50 |
| CS-2gram+LM-Web | 15.32 |
| CS-3gram+LM-Web | 15.26 |
| Boost-2gram+CS-2gram+LM-Web | 15.39 |
| Boost-3gram+CS-3gram+LM-Web | **15.78** |
| MANY+LM-ad | **15.49** |
| Boost-2gram+LM-ad | 15.24 |
| Boost-3gram+LM-ad | 15.32 |
| CS-2gram+LM-ad | 15.72 |
| **CS-3gram+LM-ad** | **15.85** |
| Boost-2gram+CS-2gram+LM-ad | 15.61 |
| Boost-3gram+CS-3gram+LM-ad | 15.74 |

Table 2: Impact of new features and the adapted LM on the combination result of six systems.

Table 2 summarizes the best experiments results by combining the best six systems on the test set. We observe that new features yield significant improvements in term of BLEU score whatever the language model used for decoding. But it is clear that the adapted LM performs relatively well in comparison with *LM-Web*, so the best gains achieved over the best single system and the baseline are respectively *1.49* and *0.71* for *CS-3-gram+LM-ad*.

## 6 Conclusion

Several technical improvements have been performed into the MT system combination MANY, that are evaluated with the BOLT project data. An adapted LM and new features gave significant gains. Previous experimental results show that using the *adapted* LM in rescoring together with word confidence score and the oldest features improves results in term of BLEU score. This even results in better translations than using a *classical* LM (*LM-Web*) trained on a monolingual training corpus.

## References

Hildebrand Almut Siljaand and Stephan Vogel. 2008. Combination of Machine Translation Systems via Hypothesis Selection from Combined N-Best Lists. *Proceedings of the Eighth Conference of the Association for Machine Translation in the Americas*, pages 254–261.

Spyros Matsoukas Antti-Veikko I. Rosti, Bing Zhang and Richard Schw. 2009. Incremental Hypothesis Alignment with Flexible Matching for Building Confusion Networks: BBN System Description for WMT09 System Combination Task. *StatMT '09 Proceedings of the Fourth Workshop on Statistical Machine Translation*, pages 61–65.

Spyros Matsoukas Antti-Veikko I.Rosti and Richard Schwartz. 2007. Improved Word-Level System Combination for Machine Translation. *Proceedings of the 45th Annual Meeting of the Association of Computational Linguistics*, pages 312–319.

Loïc Barrault. 2010. MANY Open Source Machine Translation System Combination. *The Prague Bulletin of Mathematical Linguistics*, pages 147–155.

Loïc Barrault. 2011. MANY improvements for WMT'11. *Proceedings of the Sixth Workshop on Statistical Machine Translation*, pages 135– 139.

Sanjeev Khudanpur Damianos Karakos, Jason Eisner and Markus Dreyer. 2008. Machine Translation System Combination using ITG-based Alignments. *In 46th Annual Meeting of the Association for Computational Linguistics*, pages 81–84.

Bonnie Dorr Matthew G. Snover, Nitin Madnani and Richard Schwartz. 2009. TER-Plus: Paraphrase, semantic, and alignment enhancements to translation edit rate. *Machine Translation journal*, pages 117–127.

Wade Shen, Brian Delaney, Tim Anderson, and Ray Slyh. 2008. The MIT-LL/AFRL IWSLT-2008 MT System. *In Internationnal Workshop on Spoken Language Translation*, pages 69–76.

Andreas Stolcke. 2002. Srilm-an extensible language modeling toolkit. *In Proceedings International Conference for Spoken Language Processing, Denver, Colorado.*

Nicola Ueffing and Hermann Ney. 2007. Word-Level Confidence Estimation for Machine Translation. *Computational Linguistics journal*, pages 9–40.

# Comparing CRF and template-matching in phrasing tasks within a Hybrid MT system

**George Tambouratzis**
ILSP/Athena Res. Centre
6 Artemidos & Epidavrou,
Paradissos Amaroussiou,
Athens, GR-15125, Greece.
giorg_t@ilsp.gr

## Abstract

The present article focuses on improving the performance of a hybrid Machine Translation (MT) system, namely PRESEMT. The PRESEMT methodology is readily portable to new language pairs, and allows the creation of MT systems with minimal reliance on expensive resources. PRESEMT is phrase-based and uses a small parallel corpus from which to extract structural transformations from the source language (SL) to the target language (TL). On the other hand, the TL language model is extracted from large monolingual corpora. This article examines the task of maximising the amount of information extracted from a very limited parallel corpus. Hence, emphasis is placed on the module that learns to segment into phrases arbitrary input text in SL, by extrapolating information from a limited-size parsed TL text, alleviating the need for an SL parser. An established method based on Conditional Random Fields (CRF) is compared here to a much simpler template-matching algorithm to determine the most suitable approach for extracting an accurate model. Experimental results indicate that for a limited-size training set, template-matching generates a superior model leading to higher quality translations.

## 1 Introduction

Most current MT systems translate sentences by operating at a sub-sentential level on parallel corpora. However, this frequently necessitates parsers for both SL and TL, which either (i) develop matched segmentations that give similar outputs in terms of phrasing over the SL and TL or (ii) for which a mapping is externally defined between the two given segmentations. Both alternatives limit portability to new languages, due to the need for matching the appropriate tools. Another limitation involves the amount of parallel texts needed. Statistical MT (SMT) (Koehn, 2010) generates high quality translations provided that large parallel corpora (of millions of words) are available. However, this places a strict constraint on the volume of data required to create a functioning MT system. For this reason, a number of researchers involved in SMT have recently investigated the extraction of information from monolingual corpora, including lexical translation probabilities (Klementiev et al., 2012) and topic-specific information (Su et al., 2012).

A related direction in MT research concerns hybrid MT (HMT), where principles from multiple MT paradigms are combined, such as for instance SMT and RBMT (Rule-based MT). HMT aims to combine the paradigms' positive aspects to achieve higher translation accuracy. Wu (2009) has studied the trend of convergence of MT research towards hybrid systems. Quirk et al. (2007) have proposed an HMT system where statistical principles are combined with Example-Based MT (EBMT) to improve the performance of SMT.

The PRESEMT (www.presemt.eu) methodology (Tambouratzis et. al, 2013) supports rapid development of hybrid MT systems for new language pairs. The hybrid nature of PRESEMT arises from the use of data-driven pattern recognition algorithms that combine EBMT techniques with statistical principles when modelling the target language. PRESEMT utilises a very small parallel corpus of a few hundred sentences, together with a large TL monolingual one to determine the translation. The MT process encompasses three stages:

Stage 1: this pre-processes the input sentence, by tagging and lemmatising tokens and grouping these tokens into phrases, preparing the actual translation.

Stage 2: this comprises the main translation engine, which in turn is divided into two phases:

Phase A: the establishment of the translation structure in terms of phrase order;

Phase B: the definition of word order and the resolution of lexical ambiguities at an intra-phrase level.

Stage 3: post-processing, where the appropriate tokens are generated from lemmas.

In terms of resources, PRESEMT requires:

(i) a bilingual lemma dictionary providing SL to TL lexical correspondences,

(ii) an extensive TL monolingual corpus, compiled via web crawling to generate a language model,

(iii) a very small bilingual corpus.

The bilingual corpus provides examples of the structural transformation from SL to TL. In comparison to SMT, the use of a small corpus reduces substantially the need for locating parallel corpora, whose procurement or development can be extremely expensive. Instead, a small parallel corpus can be assembled with limited recourse to costly human resources. The small size of the parallel corpus unavoidably places additional requirements on the processing accuracy in order to extract the necessary information. The main task studied here is to extract from a parallel corpus of 200 sentences appropriate structural information to describe the transformation from SL to TL. More specifically, a module needs to be trained to transfer a given TL phrasing scheme to SL, so that during translation the module segments arbitrary input text into phrases in a manner compatible to the TL phrasing scheme. The question then is which method succeeds in extracting from the parallel corpus the most accurate structural knowledge, to support an effective MT system.

For transferring a TL phrasing scheme into SL, PRESEMT relies on word and phrase alignment of the parallel corpus. This alignment allows the extrapolation of a model that segments the SL text. The SL–side segmentation is limited to phrase identification, rather than a detailed syntactic analysis.

The processing of a bilingual corpus and the elicitation of the corresponding SL-to-TL phrasing information involves two PRESEMT modules:

(i) The Phrase aligner module (PAM), which performs text alignment at word and phrase level within the parallel corpus. This language-independent method identifies corresponding terms within the SL and TL sides of each sentence, and aligns the words between the two languages, while at the same time creating phrases for the non-parsed side of the corpus (Sofianopoulos et al., 2012).

(ii) The Phrasing model generator (PMG), which elicits a phrasing model from this aligned parallel corpus. PMG is trained on the aligned parallel SL – TL sentences incorporating the PAM output to generate a phrasing model. This model is then employed to segment user-specified text during translation.

A number of studies relevant to this article involve the transfer of phrasing schemes from one language to another. These studies have focussed on extrapolating information from a resource-rich to a resource-poor language. Yarowski et al. (2001) have used automatically word-aligned raw bilingual corpora to project annotations. Och and Ney (2004) use a two-stage process via a dynamic programming-type algorithm for aligning SL and TL tokens. Simard et al. (2005) propose a more advanced approach allowing non-contiguous phrases, to cover additional linguistic phenomena. Hwa et al. (2005) have created a parser for a new language based on a set of parallel sentences together with a parser in a frequently-used language, by transferring deeper syntactic structure and introducing fix-up rules. Smith et al. (2009) create a TL dependency parser by using bilingual text, a parser, and automatically-derived word alignments.

## 2 Basic functionality & design of phrasing model generator

The default PMG implementation (Tambouratzis et al., 2011) adopts the CRF model (Lafferty at el., 2001, Wallach, 2004) to chunk each input sentence into phrases. Earlier comparative experiments have established that CRF results in a higher accuracy of phrase detection than both probabilistic models (such as HMMs) and small parsers with manually-defined parsing rules. CRF has been used by several researchers for creating parsers (for instance Sha and Pereira, 2003, Tsuruoka et al., 2009).

Due to the expressiveness of the underlying mathematical model, CRF requires a large number of training patterns to extract an accurate model. Of course, the volume of training patterns is directly dependent on the size of the parallel corpus available. A more accurate CRF would require the use of a large parallel corpus, though this would compromise the portability to new language pairs. Even by moving from handling lemmas/tokens to part-of-speech tags when training the parser, to reduce the pattern space, it is hard to model accurately all possible phrase types via CRF (in particular for rarer PoS tags) via the small corpus. On the contrary, a lower complexity PMG model (hereafter termed **PMG-simple**) may well be better suited to this data. The work presented here is aimed at investigating whether a simpler PMG model can process more effectively this limited-size parallel corpus of circa 200 parallel sentences.

## 3 Detailed description of PMG-simple

### 3.1 PMG-simple Principles

PMG-simple follows a learn-by-example concept, where, based on the appearance of phrase patterns, the system learns phrases that match exactly patterns it has previously encountered. This approach is based on the widely-used template-matching algorithm (Duda et al., 2001), where the aim is to match part of the input sentence to a known phrase archetype. PMG-simple (i) does not generate an elaborate high-order statistical model for segmentation into phrases taking into account preceding and ensuing tag sequences, and (ii) cannot revise decisions so as to reach a global optimum. Instead, PMG-simple implements a greedy search algorithm (Black, 2005), using an ordered list of known phrases. Due to its simple design, it suffers a number of potential disadvantages in comparison to CRF-type approaches:

- PMG-simple only identifies exact matches to specific patterns it has previously seen (with some exceptions, as discussed below). On the contrary, more sophisticated approaches may extrapolate new knowledge. For example, let us assume that 'Aj', 'At' and 'No' represent PoS tags for adjectives, articles and nouns respectively, while 'Ac' indicates the accusative case. Then, if noun phrases (NP) [AjAc; AjAc; NoAc] and [AtAc; AjAc; NoAc] are seen in training, the unseen pattern [AtAc; AjAc; AjAc; NoAc] may be identified as a valid NP by CRF but not by PMG-simple.
- PMG-simple does not take into account the wider phrase environment in its decision.
- PMG-simple, as a greedy algorithm, does not back-track over earlier decisions and thus may settle to sub-optimal solutions.

Conversely, PMG-simple has the following advantages:

- As it relies on a simple learn-by-example process, all segmentation decisions are easily explainable, in contrast to CRF.
- The template-matching model is trained and operates much faster than CRF.
- Finally, modifications can be integrated to improve the base algorithm generalisation. These largely consist of incorporating linguistic knowledge to allow the template-matching approach to improve language coverage and thus address specific problems caused by the limited training data.

### 3.2 PMG-simple Steps

PMG-simple receives as input the SL-side sentences of a bilingual corpus, segmented into phrases. Processing consists of four main steps:

- Step 1-<u>Accumulate & count</u>: Each sentence of the bilingual corpus is scanned in turn, using the phrases of the SL-side as training patterns. More specifically, all SL-side occurring phrases are recorded in a phrase table together with their frequency-of-occurrence in the corpus.

- Step 2-<u>Order</u>: The table is ordered, based on an ordering criterion so that phrases with a higher likelihood of correct detection are placed nearer the top of the phrase table. As a consequence, matches are initially sought for these phrases.

- Step 3-<u>Generalise</u>: Recorded phrases are generalised, to increase the phrase table coverage. Thus, new valid templates are incorporated in the phrase table, which are missing from the limited-size training corpus. Currently, generalisation involves extending phrases for which all declinable words have the same case, to other cases. For instance, if NP [AtAc; AjAc; NoAc], with all tokens in accusative exists in the phrase table with a given score, NPs are also created for nominative, genitive and vocative cases ([AtNm; AjNm; NoNm] [AtGe; AjGe; NoGe] and [AtVo; AjVo; NoVo]), with the same score.

- Step 4-Remove: Phrases containing patterns which are grammatically incorrect are removed from the phrase table. As an example of this step, phrases involving mixed cases are removed in the present implementation.

Steps 3 and 4 allow the incorporation of language-specific knowledge to enhance the operation of PMG-simple. However, in the experiments reported in the present article, only limited knowledge has been introduced, to evaluate how effective this phrasing model is in a setup where the system is not provided with large amounts of linguistic knowledge. It is expected that by providing more language-specific knowledge, the phrasing accuracy can be further increased over the results reported here.

When PMG-simple is trained, it is likely that some phrase boundaries are erroneously identified in the training data. The likelihood of such an event is non-negligible as phrases are automatically transferred using the alignment algorithm from the TL-side to the SL-side. Errors may be attributed to limited lexicon coverage or only partial correspondence of SL-to-TL text. However, as a rule such errors can be expected to correspond mainly to infrequent phrases.

A mechanism for screening such errors has been introduced in PMG-simple. This is implemented as a threshold imposed on the number of occurrences of a phrase within the training corpus, normalised over the occurrences in the entire corpus of the phrase tag sequence. Thus, phrases identified very rarely in comparison to the occurrences of their respective tag sequence are penalised as unreliable. They are retained in the phrase table, but are demoted to much lower positions. This processing of the phrase table is performed after Step 4 and represents the optional final step (Step 5) of PMG-simple.

### 3.3 Ordering Criteria

The choice of template-ordering criterion dictates the order in which phrases are matched to the input text. Since PMG-simple performs no backtracking, the actual ordering affects the segmentation accuracy substantially. A variety of different criteria have been investigated for establishing the order of precedence with which phrases are searched for. Out of these, only a selection is presented here due to space restrictions, focussing on the most effective criteria. These are depicted in Table 1.

| | |
|---|---|
| **crit.1** | If phrase_freq ≥ freq_thres :<br>Crit1 = {[(1000*(phrase_freq/ tagseq_occur) + phrase_len*250] }<br>If phrase_freq < freq_thres:<br>Crit1 = {[phrase_len *10] } |
| **crit.2** | If phrase_freq ≥ freq_thres :<br>Crit2 ={(phrase_freq[p_index]) + phrase_len*10000}<br>If phrase_freq < freq_thres:<br>Crit2 = {phrase_len *10 +floor(100*phrase_freq/ tagseq_occur)} |
| **crit.3** | If phrase_freq ≥ freq_thres :<br>Crit3 = {phrase_freq + phrase_len*1000}<br>If phrase_freq < freq_thres:<br>Crit3 ={phrase_len + phrase_freq/tagseq_occur} |
| **crit.4** | If phrase_freq ≥ freq_thres :<br>Crit4 = max {phrase_subfreq + phrase_len*100 }<br>If phrase_freq < freq_thres:<br>Crit4 = {phrase_len + phrase_subfreq/tagseq_occur} |

Table 1: Definitions of phrase-ordering criteria.

Basically, the information according to which phrases may be ordered in the phrase table consists of two types, (i) the frequency of occurrence of a given phrase in the training corpus (denoted as *phrase_freq*) and (ii) the phrase length in terms of tokens (denoted as *phrase_len*). By combining these two sources of information, different criteria are determined. Parameter *tagseq_occur* corresponds to the number of occurrences of the phrase tag sequence within the training corpus. Finally *phrase_subfreq* is equal to the occurrences of a tag sequence as either an entire phrase or as a sub-part of a larger phrase. This takes into account in the frequency calculations the instances of phrases which in turn are encapsulated within larger phrases, and is the main point of difference between criteria crit3 and crit4.

To summarise a series of earlier experiments involving different criteria, criteria using only one source of information prove to be less effective. Also, criteria using non-linear combinations of information types (i) and (ii) have been shown to be less effective and are not reported here. All criteria studied in the present article combine the two aforementioned types of information in a weighted sum, but using different multiplication factors to emphasise one information type over the other. The actual factors may of course be further optimised, as the values reported in Table 1 are chosen to differ in terms of order of magnitude.

All criteria reported here implement Step 5, by having a secondary formulation when the occurrences of a phrase fall below a threshold (parameter *freq_thres*). This results in assigning a lower priority to very infrequent phrases.

A mechanism has also been introduced for the proper handling of tokens with very infrequent part-of-speech (PoS) tags, which typically have a rate-of-appearance of less than 0.5% in the corpus. For such tags, the likelihood of appearing in the 200 parallel sentences is very low. Hence, in order to split them appropriately into phrases when they appear in input sentences, equivalence classes have been defined. A limited number of PoS equivalences are used, namely (i) abbreviations and foreign words are considered equivalent to nouns, (ii) numerals are considered equivalent to adjectives and (iii) pronouns are considered equivalent to nouns. This information is inserted in Step 3 of the phrase-ordering algorithm, allowing the generation of the appropriate phrases. Though the improvement in translation accuracy by introducing these PoS equivalences is not spectacular (no more than 0.005 BLEU points) this generalisation information allows the appropriate handling of unseen tag sequences during translation, leading to a more robust phrasing method.

It should be noted here that a non-greedy variant of PMG-simple has also been examined. This was expected to be more effective, since it extends the template matching approach to take into account a sentence-wide context. However, it has turned out that the complexity of the non-greedy approach is too high. By introducing backtracking, it becomes extremely expensive computationally to run this method for sentences larger than 12 tokens without a substantial pruning of the search space.

## 4 Experimental setup and results

### 4.1 Experiment Definition

To evaluate the proposed phrasing generator, the output of the entire translation chain up to the final translation result is studied. This allows the contribution of different PMG models to be quantified using objective metrics. For the purposes of the present article, the language pair Greek-to-English (denoted as EL→EN) is employed. Since the SL phrasing generated by PMG is based on the TL phrasing scheme, the phrase labels of the resulting SL phrases are inherited from the TL ones. In the experiments reported here (with English as TL), the TreeTagger parser (Schmid, 1994) is used. Thus the SL-side phrase types include PC, VC, ADVC and ADJC. As TreeTagger also allows for certain words (such as conjunctions) to remain outside phrases, it is possible that isolated words occur in SL too. For the purposes of modelling such occurrences, these words form single-token phrases, denoted as ISC (i.e. ISolated word Chunk).

Both the parallel corpus and the evaluation dataset employed here have been established in the PRESEMT project, and are available over the web (cf. www.presemt.eu/data). The parallel corpus has been retrieved from the web (from an EU website discussing the history of the Union), with an average size of 18 words per sentence, while the smallest sentence comprises 4 words and the largest 38 words. Only minimal editing was performed in the parallel corpus, to ensure parallelism between SL and TL. The evaluation set comprises 200 isolated sentences, each with a single reference translation (Sofianopoulos et al., 2012). These sentences have been drawn from the internet via web crawling, being required to have a length of between 7 and 40 tokens each.

### 4.2 Experimental Results for PMG-simple

Table 2 contains the translation accuracy results obtained with PMG-simple using the criteria of Table 1. In all experiments, the results concern the objective evaluation of the final translation, using four of the most widely used objective evaluation metrics, namely BLEU, NIST, TER and METEOR (NIST, 2002, Papineni et al., 2002 & Snover et al., 2006). For TER a lower value indicates a more successful translation while for other metrics, a higher value corresponds to a better translation. Since other components of the MT implementation do not change, this set of metrics provides an accurate end-to-end measurement of the effect of the phrasing model on the translation process. As can be seen from Table 2, all four criteria result in translations of a comparable accuracy. For instance, the variation between the lowest and highest BLEU scores is approximately 1%, while for the other metrics this variation is even lower.

| Criterion | BLEU | NIST | METEOR | TER |
|---|---|---|---|---|
| crit 1 | 0.3643 | 7.3153 | 0.4009 | 48.486 |
| crit 2 | 0.3679 | 7.2991 | 0.4009 | 48.590 |
| crit 3 | 0.3667 | 7.2937 | 0.4002 | 48.730 |
| crit 4 | 0.3637 | 7.2730 | 0.3980 | 48.834 |

Table 2: Translation accuracy for EL→EN, using PMG-simple with various criteria.

| cut-off freq. | BLEU | NIST | METEOR | TER |
|---|---|---|---|---|
| 0 | 0.3637 | 7.2730 | 0.3980 | 48.834 |
| 1 | 0.3637 | 7.2730 | 0.3980 | 48.834 |
| 2 | 0.3732 | 7.3511 | 0.4017 | 48.138 |
| 3 | 0.3660 | 7.2911 | 0.4007 | 48.590 |

Table 3: Translation scores for EL→EN, using PMG-simple with criterion 4 and various cut-off frequencies.

A potential for optimisation concerns the cut-off frequency (*freq_thres*) below which a phrase is considered exceptionally infrequent and is handled differently. Indicative results are shown for the four metrics studied in Table 3. As can be seen, the best results are obtained with a cut-off frequency of 2, for the given parallel corpus. Of course, this value is to an extent dependent on the training set. However, based on detailed analyses of the experimental results, it has been found that phrases that represent hapax legomena (i.e. phrases which occur only once) are not reliable for chunking purposes. Here, there are two possible explanations: (i) either such phrases represent spurious chunkings resulting from errors in the automatic alignment or (ii) they represent very infrequent phrases which again should not bias the phrasing process disproportionately. In both cases, the activation of the cut-off frequency improves the translation accuracy.

### 4.3 Comparison of PMG-simple to CRF

Of course it is essential to examine how PMG-simple translation results compare to those obtained when PRESEMT is run with the standard CRF-based phrasing model. These results are shown in Table 4. As can be seen the optimal performance of PMG-simple leads to an improved translation accuracy over the best CRF-based approach, with a rise of more than 6.2% in the BLEU score. Similarly, the improvements obtained for NIST and Meteor by introducing PMG-simple in PRESEMT are 2.1% and 2.5%, respectively. Finally, in the case of TER, for which a lower score reflects a better translation, the score is reduced by circa 3.3%. Thus, based on the results quoted in Table 3, the performance of PMG-simple is superior to that of the CRF-based system for all four metrics reported. The higher performance of PMG-simple is in agreement to the observation that - as recently reported for other applications (Mao at al., 2013) - improvements over the performance of CRF and SVM are possible by appropriately weighing templates.

| PMG | BLEU | NIST | METEOR | TER |
|---|---|---|---|---|
| PMG-simple (crit.4) | 0.3732 | 7.3511 | 0.4017 | 48.138 |
| CRF | 0.3513 | 7.1966 | 0.3919 | 49.774 |

Table 4: Translation accuracy for EL→EN, using PMG-simple with crit.4 and using CRF.

To evaluate in more detail the results of Table 4, a preliminary statistical analysis was performed. More specifically, the scores in BLEU, NIST and TER for each of the 200 test sentences were collected. For each of these metrics, a paired T-test was performed comparing the measurements obtained with (i) PMG-simple using criterion crit.4 and (ii) CRF, over each sentence. It was found that the difference in means between the BLEU populations was indeed statistically significant at a 0.05 level. In the cases of TER and NIST measurements, though, there was no statistically significant difference in the two populations.

## 5 Conclusions

PMG-simple has been proposed as a straightforward implementation to derive a phrasing model for SL text, based on template-matching. This operates on the same aligned corpus as the default CRF model, but is faster to train and has a more transparent operation. The results of PMG-simple have been compared to those of CRF, using the final PRESEMT translation output to gauge the phrasing effectiveness. The best results for PMG-simple are comfortably superior to those of CRF for all MT objective metrics used. This indicates that PMG-simple has a sufficiently high functionality. Though the modelling power of CRF is higher, the template-matching approach of PMG-simple is better harmonised to the amount of training data available. Thus PMG-simple appears to be the phrase generator of choice for PRESEMT.

One point that warrants further experimentation (currently under way) concerns the scaling-up effect of larger parallel corpora on the comparative performance of the models. Preliminary results with bilingual corpora of approximately 500 sentences have shown that the performance using PMG-simple remains superior to that with CRF, resulting in a difference of approx 0.02 for BLEU (equivalent to a 5%-6% improvement over the CRF baseline). In addition, PMG-simple has been shown to perform better than CRF when applied to the latest versions of PRESEMT, which are currently being tested and lie beyond the scope of this article.

Another topic of interest is to determine whether new improved criteria can be established. This is the subject of ongoing research.

In addition, an open question is whether the conclusions of this study are applicable to other thematic areas. In other words, could an approach such as PMG-simple be preferable to CRF in other applications involving relatively sparse data? It appears from the results summarised here that this could indeed be the case, though this remains the subject of future research.

## Acknowledgements

The author wishes to acknowledge the invaluable help of Ms. Marina Vassiliou and Dr. Sokratis Sofianopoulos, both of ILSP/Athena R.C., in integrating PMG-simple within the PRESEMT prototype and performing a number of experiments.
The research leading to these results has received funding from the POLYTROPON project (KRIPIS-GSRT, MIS: 448306).

## References

Paul E. Black. 2005. Dictionary of Algorithms and Data Structures. U.S. National Institute of Standards and Technology (NIST).

Richard O. Duda, Peter E. Hart and David G. Stork. 2001. *Pattern Classification (2nd edition).* Wiley Interscience, New York, U.S.A.

Rebecca Hwa, Philip Resnik, Amy Weinberg, Clara Cabezas and Okan Kolak. 2005. Bootstrapping parsers via Syntactic Projections across Parallel Texts. *Natural Language Engineering*, Vol. 11, pp. 311-325.

Alexandre Klementiev, Ann Irvine, Chris Callison-Burch and David Yarowsky. 2012. Towards Statistical Machine Translation without Parallel Corpora. *In Proceedings of EACL-2012 Conference*, Avignon, France, 23-25 April, pp. 130-140.

Philip Koehn. 2010. *Statistical Machine Translation.* Cambridge University Press, Cambridge.

John Lafferty, Andrew McCallum, and Fernando Pereira. 2001. Conditional Random Fields: Probabilistic Models for Segmenting and Labelling Sequence Data, *In Proceedings of ICML Conference*, June 28-July 1, Williamstown, USA, pp. 282-289.

Qi Mao, and Ivor Wai-Hung Tsang. 2013. Efficient Multitemplate Learning for Structured Production. *IEEE Transactions on Neural Networks and Learning Systems*, Vol. 24, No. 2, pp. 248-261.

NIST 2002. Automatic Evaluation of Machine Translation Quality Using n-gram Co-occurrences Statistics.

Franz Josef Och and Hermann Ney. 2004. The Alignment Template Approach to Statistical Machine Translation. *Computational Linguistics*, Vol. 30, No. 4, pp. 417-449.

Kishore Papineni, Salim Roukos, Todd Ward, and Wei-Jing Zhu. 2002. BLEU: A Method for Automatic Evaluation of Machine Translation. Proceedings of the *$40^{th}$ ACL Meeting*, Philadelphia, USA, pp. 311-318.

Chris Quirk and Arul Menezes. 2006. Dependency Treelet Translation: The convergence of statistical and example-based machine translation? *Machine Translation*, Vol. 20, pp. 43–65.

Helmut Schmid. 1994. Probabilistic Part-of-Speech Tagging Using Decision Trees. *In Proceedings of International Conference on New Methods in Language Processing*, Manchester, UK, pp. 44-49.

Fei Sha and Fernando C. N. Pereira. 2003. Shallow Parsing with Conditional Random Fields. I*n Proceedings of HLT-NAACL Conference*, pp. 213-220.

Michel Simard, Nicola Cancedda, Bruno Cavestro, Marc Dymetman, Eric Gaussier, Cyril Goutte, Kenji Yamada, Philippe Langlais, and Arne Mauser. 2005. Translating with Non-Contiguous Phrases. *In Proceedings of the Conferences on Human Language Technology and on Empirical Methods in Language Processing*, Vancouver, Canada, pp. 755-762.

Matthew Snover, Bonnie Dorr, Richard Schwartz, Linnea Micciulla, and John Makhoul. 2006. A Study of Translation Edit Rate with Targeted Human Annotation. *Proceedings of the 7th Conference of the Association for Machine Translation in the Americas*, Cambridge, Massachusetts, USA, pp. 223-231.

Sokratis Sofianopoulos, Marina Vassiliou, and George Tambouratzis. 2012. Implementing a language-independent MT methodology. *In Proceedings of the First Workshop on Multilingual Modeling*, held within the ACL-2012 Conference, Jeju, Republic of Korea, 13 July, pp.1-10.

Jinsong Su, Hua Wu, Haifeng Wang, Yidong Chen, Xiaodong Shi, Huailin Dong and Qun Liu. 2012. Translation Model Adaptation for Statistical Machine Translation with Monolingual Topic Information. *In Proceedings of the 50th ACL Meeting*, Jeju, Republic of Korea, pp. 459-468.

George Tambouratzis, Fotini Simistira, Sokratis Sofianopoulos, Nikolaos Tsimboukakis, and Marina Vassiliou. 2011. A resource-light phrase scheme for language-portable MT. *In Proceedings of the 15th EAMT Conference*, 30-31 May, Leuven, Belgium, pp. 185-192.

George Tambouratzis, Michalis Troullinos, Sokratis Sofianopoulos, and Marina Vassiliou. 2012. Accurate phrase alignment in a bilingual corpus for EBMT systems. *In Proceedings of the 5th BUCC Workshop*, held within the LREC-2012 Conference, May 26, Istanbul, Turkey, pp. 104-111.

George Tambouratzis, Sokratis Sofianopoulos, and Marina Vassiliou (2013) Language-independent hybrid MT with PRESEMT. *In Proceedings of HYTRA-2013 Workshop*, held within the ACL-2013 Conference, Sofia, Bulgaria, 8 August, pp. 123-130.

Yoshimasa Tsuruoka, Jun'ichi Tsujii and Sophia Ananiadou. 2009. Fast Full Parsing by Linear-Chain Conditional Random Fields. *In Proceedings of the 12th EACL Conference*, Athens, Greece, 30 March-3 April, pp. 790–798.

Hanna M. Wallach. 2004. Conditional Random Fields: An Introduction. CIS Technical Report, MS-CIS-04-21. 24 February, University of Pennsylvania.

Dekai Wu. 2009. Toward machine translation with statistics and syntax and semantics. *In Proceedings of the IEEE Workshop on Automatic Speech Recognition & Understanding*, 13-17 November, Merano, Italy, pp. 12-21.

David Yarowsky and Grace Ngai. 2001. Inducing Multilingual POS Taggers and NP Bracketers via Robust Projection across Aligned Corpora. *In NAACL-2001 Conference Proceedings*, pp. 200-207.

# Controlled Authoring In A Hybrid Russian-English Machine Translation System

**Svetlana Sheremetyeva**
National Research South Ural State University / pr.Lenina 74, 454080 Chelyabinsk, Russia
LanA Consulting ApS/ Moellekrog 4, Vejby, 3210, Copenhagen, Denmark
lanaconsult@mail.dk

## Abstract

In this paper we describe the design and deployment of a controlled authoring module in REPAT, a hybrid Russian-English machine translation system for patent claims. Controlled authoring is an interactive procedure that is interwoven with hybrid parsing and simplifies the automatic stage of analysis. Implemented in a pre-editing tool the controlled authoring module can be stand-alone and pipelined to any foreign MT system. Although applied to the Russian-English language pair in the patent domain, the approach described is not specific for the Russian language and can be applied for other languages, domains and types of machine translation application.

## 1 Introduction

MT systems have become an inherent part of translation activities in spite of general understanding that it is impossible to get high quality machine translation (MT) without human judgment (Koehn, 2009). In addition to lexical ambiguity, among the linguistic phenomena that lower translatability indicators (Underwood and Jongejan, 2001) is the syntactic complexity of a source text, of which the patent claim whose sentence can run for a page or so is an ultimate example.

A wide range of activities can be found in the area of developing different techniques to "help" an MT engine cope with the ambiguity and complexity of the natural language. Recent work investigated the inclusion of interactive computer-human communication at each step of the translation process by, e.g., showing the user various "paths" among all translations of a sentence (Koehn, cf.), or keyboard-driving the user to select the best translation (Macklovitch, 2006). One of the latest publications reports on Patent statistical machine translation (SMT) from English to French where the user drives the segmentation of the input text (Pouliquen et.al, 2011). Another trend to cope with the source text complexity is to rewrite a source text into a controlled language (CL) to ensure that the MT input conforms to the desired vocabulary and grammar constraints. When a controlled language is introduced, the number of parses per sentence can be reduced dramatically compared to the case when a general lexicon and grammar are used to parse specialized domain texts.

Controlled language software is developed with different levels of automation and normally involves interactive authoring (Nyberg et al., 2003). The users (authors) have to be taught the CL guidelines in order to accurately use an appropriate lexicon and grammar during authoring. In line with these studies is the research on developing pre-editing rules, e.g., textual patterns that reformulate the source text in order to improve the source text translatability and MT output. Such rules implemented in a software formalism are applied for controlled language authoring (Bredenkamp et al. 2000; Rayner et al. 2012).

This paper focuses on the design, deployment and utilization of a controlled language in the implementation of the hybrid REPAT environment for machine translation of patent claims from Russian into English. In selecting Russian as a source language we were motivated by two major considerations. Firstly, Russia has a huge pool of patents which are unavailable for non-Russian speakers without turning to expensive translation services. The situation is of great disadvantage for international technical knowledge assimilation, dissemination, protection of inventor's rights and patenting of new inventions. Secondly, in an attempt to find ways that could lower efforts in developing MT systems involving inflecting languages, for which statistical techniques normally fail (Sharoff, 2004), we were challenged to develop a hybrid technique for parsing morphologically rich languages on the example of such a highly inflecting language as Russian.

In what follows we first give an overview of the REPAT machine translation environment and then focus on the components of the system which are responsible for controlled authoring of the source texts with complex syntactic structure, such as patent claims. These components raise the translatability of patent claims and, second, improve their readability in both source and target languages, which for patent claims is of great importance. It is well known that an extremely complex syntactic structure of the patent claim is a problematic issue for understanding (readability) even in a source language (Shinmori et al., 2003), let alone in translation.

## 2 REPAT environment overview

The REPAT system takes a Russian patent claim as input and produces translations at two major levels, the level of terminology (not just any chunks), and the text level. Full translation of a patent claim is output in two formats, - in the form of one sentence meeting all legal requirements to the claim text, and as a better readable set of simple sentences in the target language. In Figure 3 an example of the REPAT output is shown for a fragment of a Russian claim given below:

*Стеклоподъемник автомобиля содержащий электропривод и направляющую с ползуном, отличающийся тем, что в ползуне выполнены два гнезда, образованные пластиной и выемками во вкладыше, в которых расположены параллельно друг другу две цилиндрические витые пружины для компенсации вытяжки каната...*

The system also improves the readability of a source claim by decomposing it into a set of simple sentences that can be useful for a posteditor to better understand the input and thus control the quality of claim translation. The REPAT translation environment includes hybrid modules for source language analysis, controlled authoring, terminology management, knowledge development and rule-based modules for transfer and target text generation. All modules work on controlled language which is built into the system. The overall architecture of the system is shown in Figure 1. The workflow includes these main steps:

*Source claim shallow analysis based on hybrid techniques*. It serves two purposes : a) the on-the-fly translation of terminology; this can be used by a non-SL speaker for digest, and b) the preparation of a raw document for authoring in case a full claim translation is needed; the input is made interactive and the nominal and predicate terms are highlighted, the predicate terminology is linked to the knowledge base.

*Terminology update*. The document is checked against the system bilingual lexicon and unknown words are flagged. If needed the lexicon can be updated.

*Authoring*. The document is authored to conform the controlled lexicon and grammar. Unknown words are either avoided or flagged. The source claim syntactic structure is simplified. The simplification also serves the purpose of improving the readability of a source language claim.

*Document processing and translation*. This includes document parsing into a formal content representation, generation of a source claim in a controlled language, crosslinguistic transfer and generation of the target text. The full translation is output in two controlled syntax formats, a) as one complex sentence meeting all legal requirements to the claim text, and d) as a better readable set of simple sentences that might meet the needs of the user in case the translation is needed to assimilate technical knowledge rather than to be included in a patent document. The simplified syntactic presentation of translation can be useful for further automatic claim processing, e.g., when translation into other languages is needed.

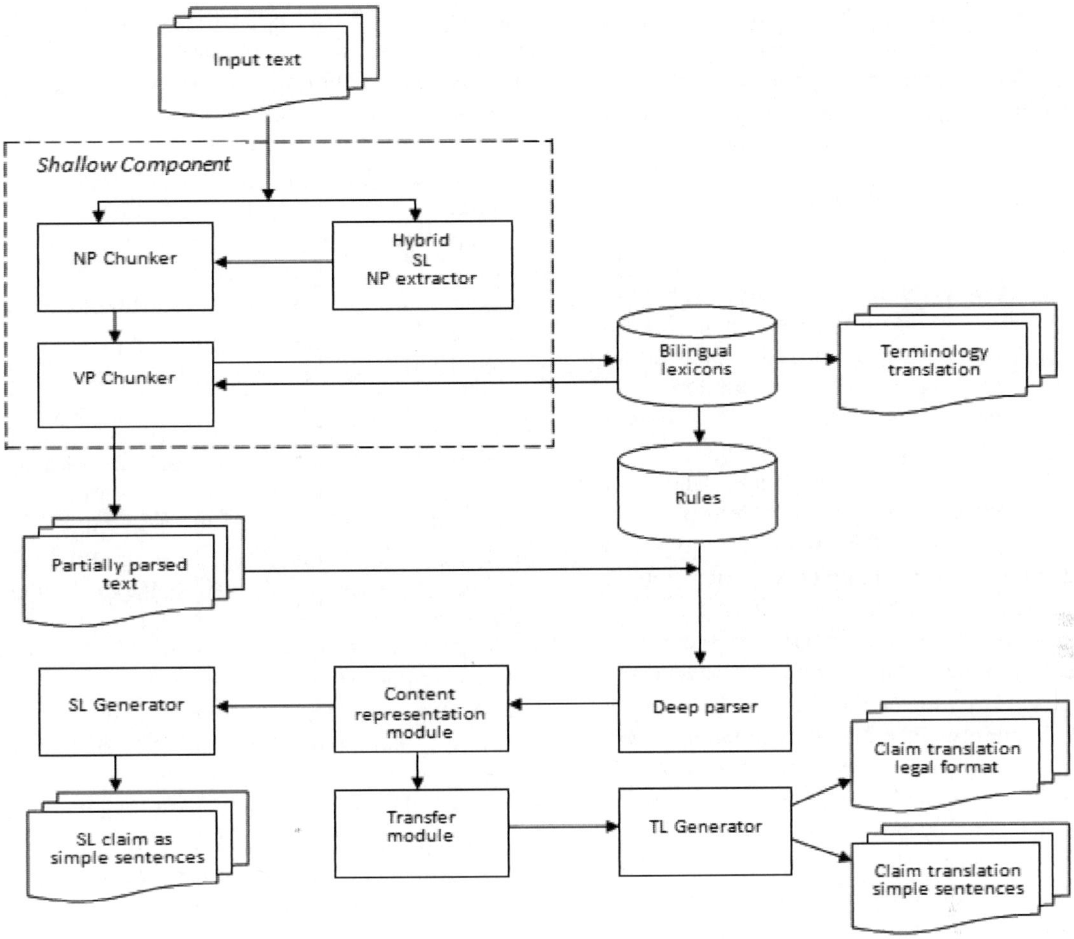


Figure 1. An overall architecture of the hybrid REPAT system.

## 3 Controlled language

The system controlled language specifies constraints on the lexicon and constraints on the complexity of sentences. It draws heavily on the patent claim sublanguage on devices in automobile industry, and in addition to the universal phenomena affecting translatability (Underwood and Jongejan, cf.) it addresses the REPAT engine-specific constraints.

Constraints of the REPAT controlled language are mainly coded in the corpus-based system lexicon, where ambiguous terms, that unavoidably emerge in any doimain are split in different lexemes, each having only one domain meaning. Where possible ambiguous lexemes are put in the lexicon as components of longer terms/phrases with one meaning. To disambiguate the residue of ambiguous terms we have created a method for disambiguation of lexical items that supports interactive disambiguation by the user through the system user interface.

Grammar restrictions on the structure of sentences are set by an implicitly controlled grammar which is associated with a controlled set of predicate/argument patterns in the system lexicon rather than with syntactic sentence-level constraints. The patterns code domain-based information on the most frequent co-occurrences of predicates in finite forms with their case-roles, as well as their linear order in the claim text. For example, the pattern (1 x 3 x 2) corresponds to such clam fragment as

1:*boards* x: *are* 3:*rotatably* x: *mounted* 2: *on the pillars*

The controlled language restrictions are imposed on the source text semi-automatically. The system prompts the user to make correct authoring decisions by providing structural templates from the system knowledge base and by raising the users' awareness about the linguistic phenomena that can increase the potential problems in machine translation. For example, the users are encouraged to repeat a preposition or a noun in conjoined constructions, limit the use of pronouns and conjunctions, put participles specifying a noun in postposition, etc.

## 4 Analyzer and authoring engine

Authoring engine is interwoven with the system hybrid analyzer. The analyzer performs two tasks in the REPAT system. It analyzers the input text into a formal internal representation and provides environment for authoring. In particular, the analyzer performs the following authoring-related steps:

*Segmentation and lexicalization.* The input text is chunked into noun phrases (NPs) predicate phrases (VPs) and other types of lexical units. Every chunk is lexicalized by associating it with a known lexicon entry.

The source NPs are chunked based on the dynamic knowledge automatically produced by a stand-alone hybrid extractor, the core of the REPAT shallow parsing component. It was ported to the Russian language following the methodology of NP extraction for English described in (Sheremetyeva 2009). The extraction methodology combines statistical techniques, heuristics and a shallow linguistic knowledge. The extractor does not rely on a preconstructed corpus, works on small texts, does not miss low frequency units and can reliably extract all NPs from an input text. The extraction results do not deteriorate when the extraction methodology is applied to inflecting languages (Russian in our case).

The NPs are chunked by matching the extractor output (lists the source claim NPs in their text form) against the claim text. Here the language rich inflection properties turn to be an advantage: the NP chunking procedure proves to be very robust with practically no ambiguity. NPs excluded, the rest of the claim lexica is chunked by the lexicon look-up practically without (ambiguity) problems. The analyzer thus trigs highlighting of the nominal and verbal terminology, flags unknown words and provides means for lexical disambiguation. All lexicalized chunks are tagged with supertags coding sets of typed features as found in the morphological zones of the lexicon.

*Automatic and Interactive Disambiguation.* Ambiguity of lexical units are resolved, either via a) automatic selection of the most likely meaning, using a set of disambiguation heuristics, or b) interactive clarification with the user. Syntactic ambiguity is to be resolved by human-computer interaction with strong computer support in the form of predicate templates to be filled with claim segments.

*Content representation.* A formal internal representation of the source claim content is built in the following two steps:

Construction of the underspecified internal representations resulting from the authoring procedure of calling and filling predicate templates by the user. A predicate template is a visualization of a corresponding predicate case-role pattern in the system lexicon. The main slot in the template corresponds to the predicate, while other slots represent case-roles. By supplying fillers into the slots of predicate templates the user in fact puts syntactic borders between the argument phrases and determines the dependency relations between the predicates and their arguments.

Automatic completion of tagging and recursive chunking by the deep parser component that works over the set of the disambiguating features of the underspecified content representation. The final parse, a set of tagged predicate/argument structures, is then submitted into a) the source language generator that outputs a source claim in a more readable format of simple sentences, and b) to the transfer module and then to the target language generator, that outputs translations in two formats.

## 5 Authoring Interface

A screenshot of the REPAT authoring interface is shown in Figure 2. In the left pane it shows an interactive source claim with nominal and predicate terminology highlighted in different colours. Unknown words, if any, will be flagged. The user is encouraged not to use such words and remove the flag. In case the user considers them necessary, the flag stays (the terms are passed to the developer for lexicon update). The highlighted terminology improves the input readability and helps the user quicker and better understand the input content and structure. To simplify the input structure the user clicks on a predicate and gets a pop-up template whose slots are to be filled out with texts strings. Predicate templates are generated based on the case-role patterns in the system lexicon.

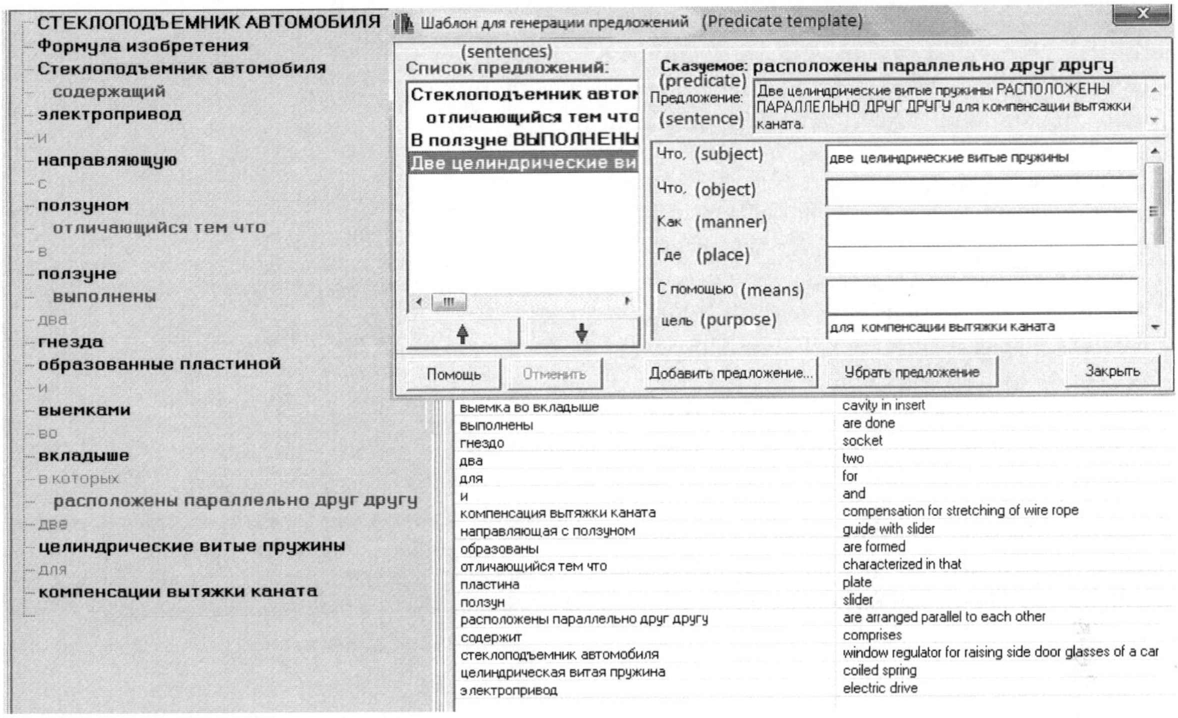


Figure 2. A screenshot of the user interface showing the authoring set up for a fragment of the Russian claim given in Section 2. The source text with visualized terms is shown in the left pane. In the middle is the template for the Russian predicate *является (is).* The English translations for the terminology are shown in the bottom of the right pane.

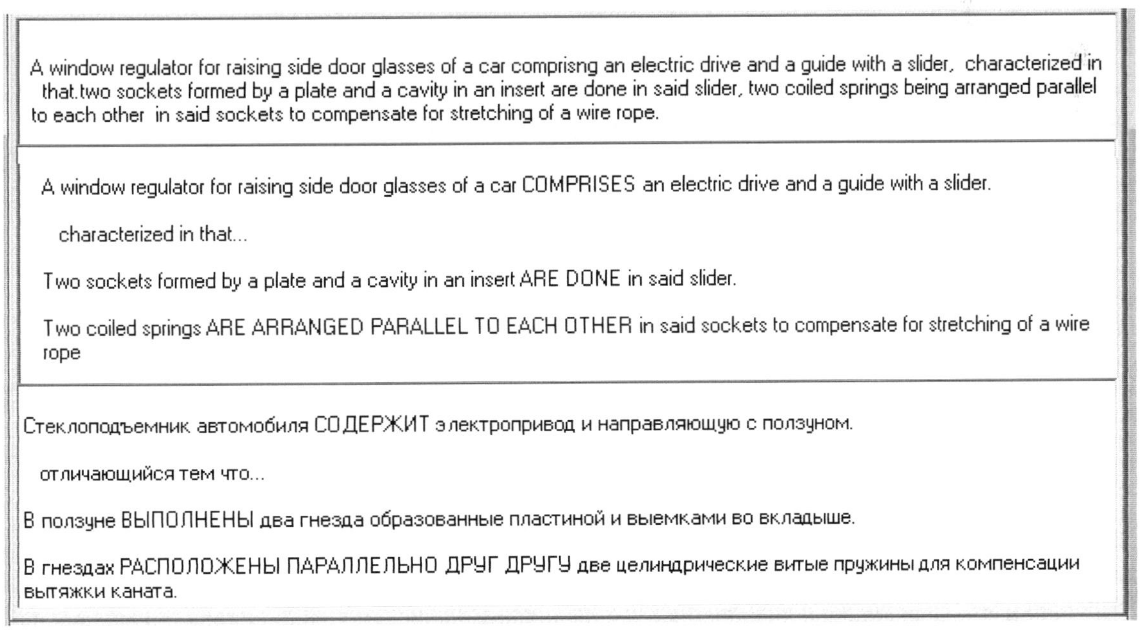


Figure 3. The two translation variants of the patent claim fragment given in Section 2. On the top the claim translation into English in the legal format of one nominal sentence is shown. In the middle the "better readable" claim translation in the form of simple sentences is displayed. In the bottom the authored Russian input text is given.

The main slot of the template is automatically filled with a predicate in a finite form, not withstanding in which form the predicate was used in the text. Other predicate slots are referenced to particular case-roles whose semantic statuses are explained to the user by the questions next to the predicate slots. The user can either drag-and-drop appropriate segments from the interactive claim text or simply type the text in the slots. During the process of filling the template the system shows translations of the lexica used in the bottom of the right pane. In case a unit put in the slot is not found in the lexicon, it is flagged. The user is encouraged to either avoid using a problematic unit or substitute it with a synonym known to the system. Once the template is filled, the system automatically generates a grammatically correct simple sentence in the source language and displays it for control. In addition to constraining the complexity of the sentence structure predicate templates also put certain constraints on the phrase level. As templates are meant for simple sentences only, coordination of verbal phrases (predicates) that may be ambiguous is avoided. Prepositions or particles attached to the verb are put to the main (predicate) template slot that resolves a possible attachment ambiguity.

The authoring procedure completed, the underspecified content representation built by the analyzer "behind the scenes" is passed to the other modules of the REPAT for translation. The authored claim in the source language can also be saved and input in any foreign MT system.

## Conclusions

We presented an authoring environment integrated in the hybrid PATMT system for translating patent claims. The efficiency of the system is conditioned by the controlled language framework. The controlled language data are created based on the domain-specific analysis of the patent corpus on devices in automobile industry. The constraints of the controlled language are embedded into the system knowledge base and included into a comprehensive, self-paced training material.

The authoring environment is interwoven with hybrid analysis components specially developed for inflecting languages. Rich morphology turns out to be an advantage in our approach. A great variety of morphological forms significantly lowers ambiguity in source text chunking and lexicalization.

The system is implemented in the programming language C++ for the Windows operational environment.

## References

Bredenkamp, A., Crysmann, B., and Petrea, M. 2000. Looking for Errors: A Declarative Formalism for Resource-Adaptive Language Checking. *Proceedings of LREC 2000.* Athens, Greece.

Koehn Philipp. 2009. A process study of computer-aided translation, *Philipp Koehn, Machine Translation Journal,* 2009, volume 23, number 4.

Macklovitch, Elliott. 2006. TransType2: The last word. *In proceedings of LREC06*, Genoa, May.

Nyberg E., T Mitamura, D. Svoboda, J. Ko, K. Baker, J. Micher 2003. An Integrated system for Source language Checking, Analysis and Terminology management. *Proceedings of Machine Translation Summit IX,* September. New-Orleans.USA

Pouliquen Bruno, Christophe Mazenc Aldo Iorio. 2011. Tapta: A user-driven translation system for patent documents based on domain-aware Statistical Machine. *Proceedings of the EAMT Conference.* Leuven, Belgium, May.

Rayner, M., Bouillon, P., and Haddow, B. 2012. Using Source-Language Transformations to Address Register Mismatches in SMT. In *Proceedings of the Conference of the Association for Machine Translation in the Americas (AMTA),* October, San Diego, USA.

Sharoff, S. 2004. What is at stake: a case study of Russian expressions starting with a preposition. In: *Proceedings of the Second ACL Workshop on Multiword Expressions Integrating Processing.*

Sheremetyeva S. 2009 On Extracting Multiword NP Terminology for MT. *Proceedings of the Thirteen Conference of European Association of Machine Translation*, Barcelona, Spain. May 14-15

Shinmori A., Okumura M., Marukawa Y. Iwayama M. 2003. Patent Claim Processing for Readability - Structure Analysis and Term Explanation, *Workshop on Patent Corpus Processing. conjunction with ACL 2003*, Sapporo. Japan, July.

Underwood N.L. and Jongejan B. 2001. Translatability Checker: A Tool to Help Decide Whether to Use MT. *Proceedings of MT Summit VIII,* Santiago de Compostela, Spain.

# Using Feature Structures to Improve Verb Translation in English-to-German Statistical MT

**Philip Williams**[⋆]
p.j.williams-2@sms.ed.ac.uk
School of Informatics[⋆]
University of Edinburgh

**Philipp Koehn**[⋆†]
pkoehn@inf.ed.ac.uk
Center for Speech and Language Processing[†]
The Johns Hopkins University

## Abstract

SCFG-based statistical MT models have proven effective for modelling syntactic aspects of translation, but still suffer problems of overgeneration. The production of German verbal complexes is particularly challenging since highly discontiguous constructions must be formed consistently, often from multiple independent rules. We extend a strong SCFG-based string-to-tree model to incorporate a rich feature-structure based representation of German verbal complex types and compare verbal complex production against that of the reference translations, finding a high baseline rate of error. By developing model features that use source-side information to influence the production of verbal complexes we are able to substantially improve the type accuracy as compared to the reference.

## 1 Introduction

Syntax-based models of statistical machine translation (SMT) are becoming increasingly competitive against state-of-the-art phrase-based models, even surpassing them for some language pairs. The incorporation of syntactic structure has proven effective for modelling reordering phenomena and improving the fluency of target output, but these models still suffer from problems of overgeneration.

One example is the production of German verbal constructions. This is particularly challenging for SMT models since highly discontiguous constructions must be formed consistently, often from multiple independent rules. Whilst the model's grammar may contain rules in which a complete multi-word verb translation is captured in a single discontiguous rule, in practice many verb translations are incompletely or inconsistently produced.

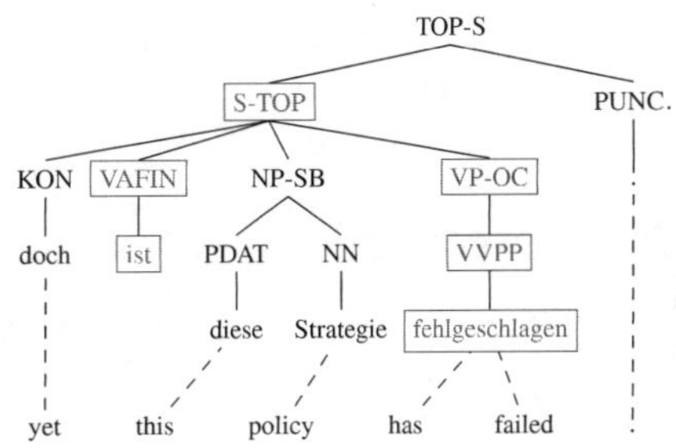


Figure 1: Alignment graph for a sentence pair from the training data. The boxes indicate the components of the target-side verbal complex: a main verb, *fehlgeschlagen*, and an auxiliary, *ist*.

There are many routes by which ill-formed constructions come to be licensed by the model, none of which is easy to address. For instance, Figure 1 shows an example from our training data in which a missing alignment link (between *has* and *ist*) allows the extraction of rules that translate *has failed* to the incomplete *fehlgeschlagen*.

Even with perfect word alignments, the extracted rules may not include sufficient context to ensure the overall grammaticality of a derivation. The extent of this problem will depend partly on the original treebank annotation style, which typically will not have been designed with translation in mind. The problem may be further exacerbated by errors during automatic parsing.

In this paper, we address the problem by focusing on the derivation process. We extend a strong SCFG-based string-to-tree model to incorporate a rich feature-structure based representation of German verbal complex types. During decoding, our model composes type values for every clause. When we compare these values against those of the reference translations, we find a high baseline rate of error (either incomplete or mismatching values). By developing model features that use source-side information to influence the production of verbal complexes we are able to substantially improve the type accuracy as compared to the reference.

## 2 Verbal Complex Structures

Adopting the terminology of Gojun and Fraser (2012), we use the term 'verbal complex' to mean a main verb and any associated auxiliaries within a single clause.

### 2.1 Feature Structures

We use feature structures to represent the underlying grammatical properties of German verbal complexes. The feature structures serve two main functions: the first is to specify a type for the verbal complex. The types describe clause-level properties and are defined along four dimensions: 1. tense (present, past, perfect, pluperfect, future, future perfect), 2. voice (active, werden-passive, sein-passive), 3. mood (indicative, subjunctive I, subjunctive II), and 4. auxiliary modality (modal, non-modal).

The second function is to restrict the choice of individual word forms that are allowed to combine within a given type. For example, a feature structure value for the verbal complex *hat ... gespielt* belongs to the perfect, active, indicative, non-modal type. Additionally, it specifies that for this type, the verbal complex comprises exactly two verbs: one is a finite, indicative form of the auxiliary *haben* or *sein*, the other is a past-participle.

### 2.2 The Lexicon

Our model uses a lexicon that maps each German verb in the target-side terminal vocabulary to a set of features structures. Each feature structure contains two top-level features: POS, a part-of-speech feature, and VC, a verbal complex feature of the form described above.

Since a verbal complex can comprise multiple individual verbs, the lexicon entries include partial VC structures. The full feature structure values are composed through unification during decoding.

VP-OC $\rightarrow \langle$ *rebuilt* , *wieder aufgebaut* $\rangle$
$\langle$ VP-OC VC $\rangle = \langle$ *aufgebaut* VC $\rangle$
$\langle$ *aufgebaut* POS $\rangle =$ VVPP

S-TOP $\rightarrow \langle$ X$_1$ *have* X$_2$ *been* X$_3$ ,
PP-MO$_1$ *wurde* NP-SB$_2$ VP-OC$_3$ $\rangle$
$\langle$ S-TOP VC $\rangle = \langle$ *wurde* VC $\rangle$
$\langle$ S-TOP VC $\rangle = \langle$ VP-OC VC $\rangle$
$\langle$ *wurde* POS $\rangle =$ VAFIN

Figure 2: SCFG rules with constraints

The lexicon's POS values are derived from the parse trees on the target-side of the training data. The VC values are assigned according to POS value from a small set of hand-written feature structures. Every main verb is assigned VC values from one of three possible groups, selected according to whether the verb is finite, a past-participle, or an infinitive. For the closed class of modal and non-modal auxiliary verbs, VC values were manually assigned.

## 3 The Grammar

Our baseline translation model is learned from a parallel corpus with automatically-derived word alignments. In the literature, string-to-tree translation models are typically based on either synchronous context-free grammars (SCFGs) (as in Chiang et al. (2007)) or tree transducers (as in Galley et al. (2004)). In this work, we use an SCFG-based model but our extensions are applicable in both cases.

Following Williams and Koehn (2011), each rule of our grammar is supplemented with a (possibly-empty) set of PATR-II-style identities (Shieber, 1984). Figure 2 shows two example rules with identities. The identities should be interpreted as constraints that the feature structures of the corresponding rule elements are compatible under unification. During decoding, this imposes a hard constraint on rule application.

### 3.1 Identity Extraction

The identities are learned using the following procedure:

1. The syntax of the German parse trees is used to identify verbal complexes and label the participating verb and clause nodes.

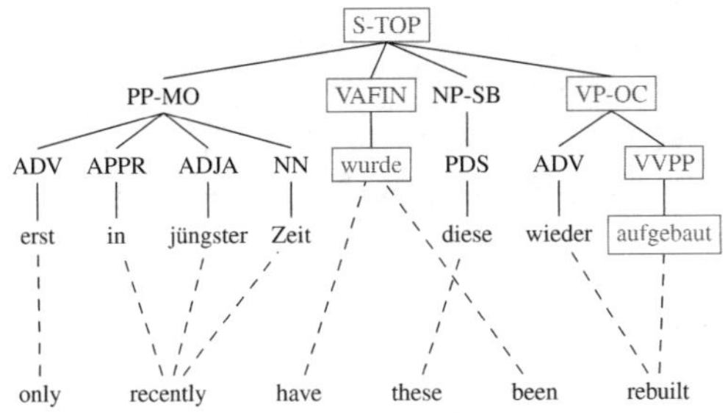


Figure 3: Alignment graph for a sentence pair from the training data. The target sentence has a single verbal complex. Participating nodes are indicated by the boxes.

2. Grammar rule extraction is extended to generate identities between VC values when an SCFG rule contains two or more nodes from a common verbal complex.

3. POS identities are added for terminals that appear in VC identities.

Figure 3 shows a sentence-pair from the training data with the verbal complex highlighted. The rules in Figure 2 were extracted from this sentence-pair.

Crucially, in step 2 of the extraction procedure the identities can be added to SCFG rules that cover only part of a verbal complex. For example, the first rule of Figure 2 includes the main verb but not the auxiliary. On application of this rule, the partial VC value is propagated from the main verb to the root. The second rule in Figure 2 identifies the VC value of an auxiliary with the VC value of a VP-OC subderivation (such as the subderivation produced by applying the first rule).

## 4 Source-side Features

Since Och and Ney (2002), most SMT models have been defined as a log-linear sum of weighted feature functions. In this section, we define two verbal-complex-specific feature functions. In order to do so, we first describe 'clause projection,' a simple source-syntactic restriction on decoding. We then describe our heuristic method of obtaining probability estimates for a target verbal complex value given the source clause.

### 4.1 Clause Projection

Our feature functions assume that we have an alignment from source-side clauses to target clauses. In order to satisfy this requirement, we adopt a simple restriction that declarative clauses (both main and embedded) on the source-side must be translated as clauses on the target-side. This is clearly an over-simplification from a linguistic perspective but it appears not to harm translation quality in practice. Table 1 shows small gains in BLEU score over our baseline system with this restriction.

| Test Set | Baseline | Clause Proj. | |
|---|---|---|---|
| newstest2008 | 15.7 | 15.8 | (+0.1) |
| newstest2009 | 14.9 | 15.0 | (+0.1) |
| newstest2010 | 16.5 | 16.8 | (+0.3) |
| newstest2011 | 15.4 | 15.5 | (+0.1) |

Table 1: Results with and without clause projection (baseline tuning weights are used for clause projection)

Clause projection is implemented as follows:

1. The input sentence is parsed and a set of clause spans is extracted according to the 1-best parse. We use the Berkeley parser (Petrov and Klein, 2007), which is trained on the Penn Treebank and so we base our definition of a declarative clause on the treebank annotation guidelines.

2. We modify the decoder to produce derivations in chart cells only if the cell span is consistent with the set of clause spans (i.e. if source span [i,j] is a clause span then no derivation is built over span [m,n] where $i < m \leq j$ and $n > j$, etc.)

3. We modify the decoder so that grammar rules can only be applied over clause spans if they have a clause label ('S' or 'CS', since the parser we use is trained on the Tiger treebank).

### 4.2 Verbal Complex Probabilities

When translating a clause, the source-side verbal complex will often provide sufficient information to select a reasonable type for the target verbal complex, or to give preferences to a few candidates. By matching up source-side and target-side verbal complexes we estimate co-occurrence frequencies in the training data. To do this for all pairs in the training data, we would need to align clauses between the source and target training sentences. However, it is not crucial that we identify every last verbal complex and so we simplify the task by restricting training data to sentence pairs in which both source and target sentences are declarative sentences, making the assumption that the main clause of the source sentence aligns with the main clause of the target.

We represent source-side verbal complexes with a label that is the string of verbs and particles and their POS tags in the order that they occur in the clause, e.g. `plays_VBZ`, `is_addressing_VBZ_VBG`. The target-side feature structures are generated by identifying verbal complex nodes in the training data parse trees (as in Section 3.1) and then unifying the corresponding feature structures from the lexicon.

Many source verbal complex labels exhibit a strong co-occurrence preference for a particular target type. For example, Table 2 shows the three most frequent feature structure values for the target-side clause when the source label is `is_closed_VBZ_VBN`. The most frequent value corresponds to a non-modal, sein-passive construction in the present tense and indicative mood.

| RF | F-Structure |
|---|---|
| 0.841 | [FIN [AUX [LEMMA sein; MOOD indicative; TENSE present]]; NON-FIN [PP/SP [PP [LEMMA *]]]] |
| 0.045 | [FIN [FULL [LEMMA sein]]; NON-FIN none] |
| 0.034 | [FIN [AUX [LEMMA werden; MOOD indicative; TENSE present]]; NON-FIN [WPP [PP [LEMMA *]; WERDEN none; WORDEN none; SEIN none]]] |
| ... | ... |

Table 2: Observed values and relative frequencies (RF) for *is closed*, which was observed 44 times in the training data.

### 4.3 Feature Functions

As with the baseline features, our verbal complex-specific feature functions are evaluated for every rule application $r_i$ of the synchronous derivation. Like the language model feature, they are non-local features and so cannot be pre-computed. Unlike the baseline features, their value depends on whether the source span that the rule is applied to is a declarative clause or not.

Both features are defined in terms of $X$, the verbal complex feature structure value of the sub-derivation at rule application $r_i$.

The first feature function, $f(r_i)$, uses the source verb label, $l$, and the probability estimate, $P(X|l)$, learned from the training data:

$$f(r_i) = \begin{cases} P(X|l) & \text{if } r_i \text{ covers a clause span} \\ & \quad \text{with verb label } l \\ & \quad \text{and } c_l \geq c_{min} \\ 1 & \text{otherwise} \end{cases}$$

The probability estimates are not used for scoring if the number of training observations falls below a threshold, $c_{min}$. We use a threshold of 10 in experiments.

The second feature function, $g(r_i)$, is simpler: it penalizes the absence of a target-side finite verb when translating a source declarative clause:

$$g(r_i) = \begin{cases} exp(1) & \text{if } r_i \text{ covers a clause span} \\ & \quad \text{and } X \text{ has no finite verb} \\ 1 & \text{otherwise} \end{cases}$$

Unlike $f$, which requires the verb label to have been observed a number of times during training, $g$ is applied to all source spans that cover a declarative clause.

Dropped finite verbs are a frequent problem in our baseline model and this feature was motivated by an early version of the analysis presented in Section 5.3.

## 5 Experiments and Analysis

In preliminary experiments, we found that changes in translation quality resulting from our verb translation features were difficult to measure using BLEU. In the following experiments, we measure accuracy by comparing verbal complex values against feature structures derived from the reference sentences.

### 5.1 Setup

Our experiments use the GHKM-based string-to-tree pipeline implemented in Moses (Koehn et al., 2007; Williams and Koehn, 2012). We extend a conventional baseline model using the constraints and feature functions described earlier.

| Data Set | Reference | | | Baseline | | | Hard Constraint | | |
|---|---|---|---|---|---|---|---|---|---|
| (MC count) | F | E | Total | F | E | Total | F | E | Total |
| Dev | 95.6% | 4.4% | 100.0% | 86.1% | 13.9% | 100.0% | 87.6% | 12.4% | 100.0% |
| (633) | 637 | 29 | 666 | 545 | 88 | 633 | 559 | 79 | 638 |
| Test | 92.2% | 7.8% | 100.0% | 83.5% | 16.5% | 100.0% | 85.4% | 14.6% | 100.0% |
| (2445) | 2439 | 206 | 2645 | 2034 | 403 | 2437 | 2096 | 359 | 2455 |

Table 3: Counts of main clause VC structures that are present and contain at least a finite verb (F) versus those that are empty or absent (E). Declarative main clause counts (MC count) are given for each input set. Counts for the three test sets are aggregated.

We extracted a translation grammar using all English-German parallel data from the WMT 2012 translation task (Callison-Burch et al., 2012), a total of 2.0M sentence pairs. We used all of the WMT 2012 monolingual German data to train a 5-gram language model.

The baseline system uses the feature functions described in Williams and Koehn (2012). The feature weights were tuned on the WMT newstest2008 development set using MERT (Och, 2003). We use the newstest2009, newstest2010, and newstest2011 test sets for evaluation. The development and test sets all use a single reference.

### 5.2 Main Clause Verb Errors

When translating a declarative main clause, the translation should usually also be a declarative main clause – that is, it should usually contain at least a finite verb. From manually inspecting the output it is clear that verb dropping is a common source of translation error in our baseline system. By making the assumption that a declarative main clause should *always* be translated to a declarative main clause, we can use the absence of a finite verb as a test for translation error.

By evaluating identities, our decoder now generates a trace of verbal complex feature structures. We obtain a reference trace by applying the same process of verbal complex identification and feature structure unification to a parse of our reference data. Given these two traces, we compare the presence or absence of main clause finite-verbs in the baseline and reference.

Since we do not have alignments between the clause nodes of the test and reference trees, we restrict our analysis to a simpler version of this task: the translation of declarative input sentences that contain only a single clause. To select test sentences, we first parse the source-side of the tuning and test sets. Filtering out sentences that are not declarative or that contain multiple clauses leaves 633, 699, 793, and 953 input sentences for newstest2008, 2009, 2010, and 2011, respectively.

Our baseline system evaluates constraints in order to generate a trace of feature structures but constraint failures are allowed and hypotheses are retained. Our hard constraint system discards all hypotheses for which the constraints fail. The $f$ and $g$ feature functions are not used in these experiments.

For all main clause nodes in the output tree, we count the number of feature structure values that contain finite verbs and are complete versus the number that are either incomplete or absent. Since constraint failure results in the production of empty feature structures, incompatible verbal combinations do not contribute to the finite verb total even if a finite verb is produced. We compare the counts of clause nodes with empty feature structures for these two systems against those of the reference set.

Table 3 shows total clause counts for the reference, baseline, and hard constraint system (the 'total' columns). For each system, we record how frequently a complete feature structure containing at least a finite verb is present (the F columns) or not (E).

As expected, the finite verb counts for the reference translations closely match the counts for the source sentences. The reference sets also contain verb-less clauses (accounting for 4.4% and 7.8% of the total clause counts for the dev and test sets). Verb-less clauses are common in the training data and so it is not surprising to find them in the reference sets.

Our baseline and hard constraint systems both fail to produce complete feature structures for a high proportion of test sentences. Table 4 shows the proportion of single-clause declarative source sentences for which the translation trace does not include a complete feature structure. As well as suggesting a high level of baseline failure, these results suggest that using constraints alone is insufficient.

| Test set | Ref. | Baseline | HC |
|---|---|---|---|
| newstest2008 | 0.0% | 13.9% | 11.7% |
| newstest2009 | 0.6% | 18.6% | 16.0% |
| newstest2010 | 0.0% | 14.5% | 12.5% |
| newstest2011 | 1.4% | 17.4% | 14.4% |

Table 4: Proportion of declarative single-clause sentences for which there is not a complete feature structure for the translation. Ref. is the reference and HC is our hard constraint system.

### 5.3 Error Classification

In order to verify that the incomplete feature structures indicate genuine translation errors and to understand the types of errors that occur, we manually check 100 sentences from our baseline system and classify the errors. We check the verb constructions of the sentences containing the first 50 failures in newstest2009 and the first 50 failures in newstest2011.

**Invalid Combination (27)** An ungrammatical combination of auxiliary and main verbs.
Example: *im Jahr 2007* ***hatte*** *es bereits um zwei Drittel* ***reduziert worden*** *.*

**Perfect missing aux (25)** There is a past-participle in sentence-final position, but no auxiliary verb.
Example: *der Dow Jones etwas später wieder* ***bereitgestellt*** *.*

**False positive (14)** Output is OK. In the sample this happens either because the output string is well-formed in terms of verb structure, but the tree is wrong, or because the parse of the source is wrong and the input does not actually contain a verb.

**No verb (13)** The input contains at least one verb that should be translated but the output contains none.
Example: *der universelle Charakter der Handy auch Nachteile .*

**Invalid sentence structure (13)** Verbs are present and make sense, but sentence structure is wrong
Example: *die rund hunderttausend Menschen in Besitz von ihren eigenen Chipcard Opencard in dieser Zeit , diese Kupon* ***bekommen kann*** *.*

**Inf missing aux (5)** There is an infinitive in sentence-final position, but no auxiliary verb *or* the main verb is erroneously in final position (the output is likely to be ambiguous for this error type).
Example: *die Preislisten dieser Unternehmen in der Regel nur ausgewählte Personen* ***erreichen*** *.*

**Unknown verb (2)** The input verb is untranslated.
Example: *dann* ***scurried*** *ich auf meinem Platz .*

**Werden-passive missing aux (1)** There is a werden-passive non-finite part, but no finite auxiliary verb.
Example: *die meisten geräumigen und luxuriösesten Wohnung im ersten Stock für die Öffentlichkeit* ***geöffnet worden*** *.*

In our classification, the most common individual error type in the baseline is the ungrammatical combination of verbs, at 27 out of 100. However, there are multiple categories that can be characterized as the absence of a required verb and combined these total 44 out of 100 errors. There are also some false positives and potentially misleading results in which wider syntactic errors result in the failure to produce a feature structure, but the majority are genuine errors. However, this method fails to identify instances where the verbal complex is grammatical but has the wrong features. For that, we compare accuracy against reference values.

### 5.4 Feature Structure Accuracy

If we had gold-standard feature structures for our reference sets and alignments between test and reference clauses then we could evaluate accuracy by counting the number of matches and reporting precision, recall, and F-measure values for this task. In the absence of gold reference values, we rely on values generated automatically from our reference sets. This requires accepting some level of error from parsing and verb labelling (we perform a manual analysis to estimate the degree of this problem). We also require alignments between

| Data Set | Experiment | F | E | g | m | Prec. | Recall | F1 |
|---|---|---|---|---|---|---|---|---|
| Dev | Baseline | 545 | 88 | 637 | 253 | 46.4 | 39.7 | 42.8 |
| | $f$ | 610 | 48 | 637 | 312 | 51.1 | 49.0 | 50.0 |
| | $g$ | 600 | 58 | 637 | 289 | 48.2 | 45.4 | 46.7 |
| | $f + g$ | 627 | 29 | 637 | 317 | 50.6 | 49.8 | 50.2 |
| Test | Baseline | 2034 | 403 | 2439 | 993 | 48.8 | 40.7 | 44.4 |
| | $f$ | 2370 | 224 | 2439 | 1214 | 51.2 | 49.8 | 50.5 |
| | $g$ | 2307 | 278 | 2439 | 1072 | 46.5 | 44.0 | 45.2 |
| | $f + g$ | 2437 | 145 | 2439 | 1225 | 50.3 | 50.2 | 50.2 |

Table 5: Feature structure accuracy for the development and test sets. As in Table 3, counts are given for main clause VC structures that are present and contain at least a finite verb (F) versus those that are absent or empty (E). The VC values of the output are compared against the reference values giving the number of matches (m). The counts F, m, and g, (the number of gold reference values) are used to compute precision, recall, and F1 values.

| | |
|---|---|
| Input | Bangladesh ex-PM **is denied** bail |
| Reference | Ehemaliger Premierministerin von Bangladesch **wird** Kaution **verwehrt** |
| Baseline | Bangladesch ex-PM **ist** keine Kaution |
| $f + g$ | Bangladesch ex-PM **wird** die Kaution **verweigert** |

| | |
|---|---|
| Input | the stock exchange in Taiwan **dropped** by 3.6 percent according to the local index . |
| Reference | Die Börse in Taiwan **sank** nach dem dortigen Index um 3,6 Prozent . |
| Baseline | die Börse in Taiwan die lokalen Index entsprechend um 3,6 Prozent **gesunken** . |
| $f + g$ | die Börse in Taiwan **fiel** nach Angaben der örtlichen Index um 3,6 Prozent . |

| | |
|---|---|
| Input | the commission **had been assembled** at the request of Minister of Sport Miroslav Drzeviecki . |
| Reference | Die Kommission **war** auf Anfrage von Sportminister Miroslaw Drzewiecki **zusammengekommen**. |
| Baseline | die Kommission **hatte** auf Antrag der Minister für Sport Miroslav Drzeviecki **montiert worden** . |
| $f + g$ | die Kommission **war** auf Antrag der Minister für Sport Miroslav Drzeviecki **versammelt** . |

Figure 4: Example translations where the baseline verbal complex type does not match the reference but the $f + g$ system does.

test and reference clauses. Here we make the same simplification as in Section 5.2 and restrict evaluation to single-clause declarative sentences.

We test the effect of the $f$ and $g$ features on feature structure accuracy. Their log-linear model weights were tuned by running a line search to optimize the F1 score on a subset of the newstest2008 dev set containing sentences up to 30 tokens in length (all baseline weights were fixed). For the experiments in which both features are used, we first tune the weight for $f$ and then tune $g$ with the $f$ weight fixed.

Table 5 reports feature structure accuracy for the development and test sets. On the test set, the individual $f$ and $g$ features both improve the F1 score. $f$ is effective in terms of both precision and recall, but the $g$ feature degrades precision compared to the baseline. Using both features appears to offer little benefit beyond using $f$ alone.

Compared with the baseline or using hard constraints alone (Table 3), the proportion of sentences with incomplete or inconsistent verbal complex values (column E) is substantially reduced by the $f$ and $g$ feature functions.

To estimate the false match rate, we manually checked the first 50 sentences from the 2009 test set in which one system was reported to agree with reference and the other not:

**37/50** Verb constructions are grammatical. We agree with comparisons against the reference value.

**9/50** Verb constructions are grammatical. We agree with the comparison for the test system but not the baseline.

**4/50** Verb constructions are ungrammatical or difficult to interpret in both baseline and test.

Figure 4 shows some example translations from our system.

### 5.5 BLEU

Finally, we report BLEU scores for two versions of our dev and test sets: in addition to the full data sets (Table 6), we use sub-sets that contain all source sentences up to 30 tokens in length (Table 7). There are two reasons for this: first, we expect shorter sentences to use simpler sentence structure with less coordination and fewer relative and subordinate clauses. All else being equal, we expect to see a greater degree of high-level structural divergence between complex source and target sentence structures than between simple ones. We therefore anticipate that our naive clause projection strategy is more likely to break down on long sentences. Second, we expect the effects on BLEU score to become diluted as sentence length increases, for the simple reason that verbs are likely to account for a smaller proportion of the total number of words (though this effect seems to be small: in a parse of the newstest2009-30 subset, verbs account for 14.2% of tokens; in the full set they account for 13.1%). We find that the change in BLEU is larger for the constrained test sets, but only slightly.

| Experiment | 2008 | 2009 | 2010 | 2011 |
|---|---|---|---|---|
| baseline | 15.7 | 14.9 | 16.5 | 15.4 |
| $f$ | 15.8 | 15.0 | 16.9 | 15.5 |
| $g$ | 15.9 | 15.1 | 16.9 | 15.6 |
| $f + g$ | 15.8 | 15.0 | 16.9 | 15.6 |

Table 6: BLEU scores for full dev/test sets

| Experiment | 2008 | 2009 | 2010 | 2011 |
|---|---|---|---|---|
| baseline | 16.1 | 15.7 | 16.3 | 15.1 |
| $f$ | 16.2 | 15.8 | 16.9 | 15.3 |
| $g$ | 16.4 | 15.9 | 16.9 | 15.4 |
| $f + g$ | 16.3 | 15.9 | 16.9 | 15.4 |

Table 7: BLEU scores for constrained dev/test sets (max. 30 tokens)

## 6 Related Work

The problem of verbal complex translation in English-to-German is tackled by Gojun and Fraser (2012) in the context of phrase-based SMT. They overcome the reordering limitation of phrase-based SMT by preprocessing the source-side of the training and test data to move English verbs within clauses into more 'German-like' positions. In contrast, our SCFG-based baseline model does not place any restriction on reordering distance.

Arora and Mahesh (2012) address a similar problem in English-Hindi translation. They improve a phrase-based model by merging verbs and associated particles into single tokens, thus simplifying the task of word alignment and phrase-pair extraction. Their approach relies upon the mostly-contiguous nature of English and Hindi verbal complexes. The discontiguity of verbal complexes rules out this approach for translation into German.

Our model adopts a similar constraint-based extension of SCFG to that described in Williams and Koehn (2011). In that work, constraints are used to enforce target-side agreement between nouns and modifiers and between subjects and verbs. Whilst that constraint model operates purely on the target-side, our verbal complex feature functions also take source-side information into account.

## 7 Conclusion

We have presented a model in which a conventional SCFG-based string-to-tree system is extended with a rich feature-structure based representation of German verbal complexes, a grammatical construction that is difficult for an SMT model to produce correctly. Our feature structure representation enabled us to easily identify where our baseline model made errors and provided a means to measure accuracy against the reference translations. By developing feature functions that use source-side information to influence verbal complex formation we were able to improve translation quality, measured both in terms of BLEU score where there were small, consistent gains across the test sets, and in terms of task-specific accuracy.

In future work we intend to explore the use of richer models for predicting target-side verbal complex types. For example, discriminative models that include non-verbal source features.

## Acknowledgements

We would like to thank the anonymous reviewers for their helpful feedback and suggestions. The research leading to these results has received funding from the European Union Seventh Framework Programme (FP7/2007-2013) under grant agreement 287658 (EU-BRIDGE).

## References


Karunesh Kumar Arora and R. Mahesh K. Sinha. 2012. Improving statistical machine translation through co-joining parts of verbal constructs in english-hindi translation. In *Proceedings of the Sixth Workshop on Syntax, Semantics and Structure in Statistical Translation*, pages 95–101, Jeju, Republic of Korea, July. Association for Computational Linguistics.

Chris Callison-Burch, Philipp Koehn, Christof Monz, Matt Post, Radu Soricut, and Lucia Specia. 2012. Findings of the 2012 workshop on statistical machine translation. In *Proceedings of the Seventh Workshop on Statistical Machine Translation*, pages 10–51, Montréal, Canada, June. Association for Computational Linguistics.

David Chiang. 2007. Hierarchical phrase-based translation. *Comput. Linguist.*, 33(2):201–228.

Michel Galley, Mark Hopkins, Kevin Knight, and Daniel Marcu. 2004. What's in a translation rule? In *HLT-NAACL '04*.

Anita Gojun and Alexander Fraser. 2012. Determining the placement of german verbs in english–to–german smt. In *Proceedings of the 13th Conference of the European Chapter of the Association for Computational Linguistics*, pages 726–735, Avignon, France, April. Association for Computational Linguistics.

Philipp Koehn, Hieu Hoang, Alexandra Birch, Chris Callison-Burch, Marcello Federico, Nicola Bertoldi, Brooke Cowan, Wade Shen, Christine Moran, Richard Zens, Chris Dyer, Ondřej Bojar, Alexandra Constantin, and Evan Herbst. 2007. Moses: open source toolkit for statistical machine translation. In *Proceedings of the 45th Annual Meeting of the ACL on Interactive Poster and Demonstration Sessions*, ACL '07, pages 177–180, Morristown, NJ, USA. Association for Computational Linguistics.

Franz Josef Och and Hermann Ney. 2002. Discriminative training and maximum entropy models for statistical machine translation. In *Proceedings of the 40th Annual Meeting on Association for Computational Linguistics*, ACL '02, pages 295–302, Morristown, NJ, USA. Association for Computational Linguistics.

Franz Josef Och. 2003. Minimum error rate training in statistical machine translation. In *Proceedings of the 41st Annual Meeting on Association for Computational Linguistics - Volume 1*, ACL '03, pages 160–167, Morristown, NJ, USA. Association for Computational Linguistics.

Slav Petrov and Dan Klein. 2007. Improved inference for unlexicalized parsing. In *Human Language Technologies 2007: The Conference of the North American Chapter of the Association for Computational Linguistics; Proceedings of the Main Conference*, pages 404–411, Rochester, New York, April. Association for Computational Linguistics.

Stuart M. Shieber. 1984. The design of a computer language for linguistic information. In *Proceedings of the 10th international conference on Computational linguistics*, COLING '84, pages 362–366, Stroudsburg, PA, USA. Association for Computational Linguistics.

Philip Williams and Philipp Koehn. 2011. Agreement constraints for statistical machine translation into german. In *Proceedings of the Sixth Workshop on Statistical Machine Translation*, pages 217–226, Edinburgh, Scotland, July. Association for Computational Linguistics.

Philip Williams and Philipp Koehn. 2012. Ghkm rule extraction and scope-3 parsing in moses. In *Proceedings of the Seventh Workshop on Statistical Machine Translation*, pages 388–394, Montréal, Canada, June. Association for Computational Linguistics.

# Building a Spanish-German Dictionary for Hybrid MT

**Anne Göhring**
Institute of Computational Linguistics
University of Zurich
goehring@cl.uzh.ch

## Abstract

This paper describes the development of the Spanish-German dictionary used in our hybrid MT system. The compilation process relies entirely on open source tools and freely available language resources. Our bilingual dictionary of around 33,700 entries may thus be used, distributed and further enhanced as convenient.

## 1 Introduction

Nowadays it is possible to set up a baseline SMT system for any language pair within a day, given enough parallel data, as well as the software to train and decode, is freely available. Whereas SMT systems profit from large amounts of data, following the general motto "more data is better data", the rule-based MT systems on the other hand benefit from high quality data. Developing a hybrid MT system on a rule-based architecture[1], one of our aims is to build and extend a high quality Spanish-German dictionary. We focus on the unidirectional lexical transfer from Spanish to German, as we are translating only in this direction. We want to balance the disadvantage of rule-based systems with respect to lexical coverage when compared to statistical MT systems trained on large scale corpora. To achieve this goal, we have merged existing resources into one bilingual dictionary. As a result we now have a consolidated Spanish-German dictionary of around 33,700 entries.

In the following section, we will give an overview of resources for German and Spanish related to our work. In section 3 we will explain which resources we used and how we combined them. We will also present some figures about the coverage of the resulting bilingual dictionary. Section 4 is dedicated to specific German linguistic issues we have addressed to complete our dictionary with the necessary morphological information. In the last section, we present our ideas for future work.

## 2 Related work and resources

Many monolingual and bilingual resources for Spanish and German already exist, some are publicly available, others only under license. The web services Canoo, Leo and Systran are freely accessible but prohibit any automated content extraction. Also the German wordnet GermaNet restricts its usage to the academic community. The HyghTra project develops hybrid high quality translation systems based on commercial resources provided by Lingenio, a language tool company specialized in machine translation (Babych et al., 2012).

In our project we work on similar systems but we follow a free resources and open source policy. This is the case of the open source suite of language analyzers FreeLing (Padró and Stanilovsky, 2012), which offers a Spanish dictionary that contains over 550,000 full-fledged word forms. The bilingual dictionary "ding-es-de"[2] compiled for the "ding" dictionary lookup program provides more than 21,000 entries.

Besides lexicons, other types of resources may provide us with extra material. Escartín (2012) has built a Spanish-German corpus with the specific aim to study multiword expressions in a translation context. There are larger parallel corpora like Acquis JRC, Europarl (Koehn, 2005), and MultiUN (Eisele and Chen, 2010), and also different multilingual wordnets such as BabelNet (Navigli and Ponzetto, 2012) and the Multilingual Central Repository (Gonzalez-Agirre et al., 2012).

[1] Our system is derived from Apertium/Matxin, and so is the dictionary format (see 3.1).

[2] savannah.nongnu.org/projects/ding-es-de

Yet another kind of valuable resources are the monolingual and parallel treebanks like the Spanish AnCora (Taulé et al., 2008) and IULA treebanks (Marimon et al., 2007), the German TiGer (Brants et al., 2004), the multilingual 'universal dependency treebank' (McDonald et al., 2013), and the Spanish-German SQUOIA treebank (Rios and Göhring, 2012).

All the open resources listed above have played or will play a role in building and extending our bilingual dictionary.

## 3 Compilation of a Spanish-German dictionary

### 3.1 Format

As we started our machine translation project using the Apertium/Matxin framework (Mayor et al., 2012), we adopted its dictionary format. Though the XML format is specific to our application, it is per definition easy to adapt. As shown in Fig. 1, a bilingual entry `<e>` has at least a left and a right side, `<l>` and `<r>` respectively, and this pair typically refers to a paradigm `<par>`. Furthermore, attributes can be set to whole paradigms as well as to individual entries. We have defined general and more refined paradigms to represent the German morphological classes and the features we need for generating the correct word forms.[3]

```
<e><p>
      <l>nota</l>
      <r>Bemerkung</r>
   </p><par n='NC_NN_FEM'/>
</e>
<e><p><l>nota</l>
      <r>Hinweis</r>
   </p><par n='NC_NN_MASC'/></e>
```

Figure 1: Two entries of the Spanish common noun *nota* (en: note; grade, mark).

### 3.2 Synonyms and polysemous words

Often a Spanish word has many German translations, and vice versa. This fact is of course reflected in our dictionary, where a Spanish lexical unit (a lemma of a given part-of-speech) has multiple entries, i.e. different corresponding German lexical units.

Fig. 2 shows the same example as in Fig. 1, the polysemous Spanish noun *nota*, together with German translations grouped according to the different senses. Note that the German word *Note* is not always the correct translation as it does not entail all senses: it is not a valid translation for sense 1.

nota ⇒
- Bemerkung, Hinweis, Notiz (sense 1: memo, note, notice)
- *Note*, Schulnote, Zensur (sense 2: mark, grade)
- Musiknote, *Note* (sense 3: musical note)

Figure 2: Different senses of the Spanish noun *nota* and their corresponding German translations.

On the one hand, the dictionary should contain as many word translations as possible in order to achieve a high coverage for both languages. On the other hand, the more fine-grained the choices in the lexicon are, the harder the lexical disambiguation becomes (Vintar et al., 2012). Although hand-written selection rules narrow down the choice in specific cases, machine learning approaches are required in order to make better lexical choices in general.

### 3.3 First compilation

We first merged the entries of the "ding-es-de" dictionary to the translations of the AnCora/FreeLing vocabulary we obtained by crawling the Spanish Wiktionary in 2011. Since this first compilation period, we have manually added new entries as required by the development of our MT system. At the end of 2013, the collected bilingual entries for the open classes noun, verb, adverb and adjective amounted to 25,904 (see Tab. 1).

At this point we decided to systematically extend our bilingual dictionary and evaluate its coverage . Translating from Spanish to German, we are first of all interested in the coverage of the source language Spanish. Compared to the more than 88,000 lemmas with about double as much senses contained in the DRAE[4], our bilingual dictionary covers not even 5% of the monolingual entries. But the DRAE is a reference dictionary, with certain shortcomings such as missing the newest neologisms and keeping obsolete words in its lexicon. Furthermore, it is not a free resource.

[3]See also Fig. 4 in section 4.2.

[4]Diccionario de la Real Academia Española; 22nd edition DRAE (2001); see www.rae.es.

### 3.4 Exploiting Wiktionary and BabelNet

FreeLing's Spanish lexicon contains 49,477 lemmas of common nouns and 7649 verb lemmas. Before the addition of more data, our dictionary covered only 19.44% of FreeLing's nouns and 22.9% of its verbs. Crawling the Wiktionary pages for the missing lemmas, we collected no more than 309 additional noun and 78 verb entries. Due to this marginal increase, we decided to test other sources. Through BabelNet's API we were able to extract 21,587 German translations of 13,824 Spanish common nouns. We used the morphology tool mOLIFde (Clematide, 2008) to analyze the German side of these BabelNet word pairs. We discarded those pairs that did not receive any analysis. The remaining candidate entries amount to 7149. Though we have not yet assess the quality of this material, the observed coverage gain from these potential bilingual entries looks promising. Adding entries for 5528 Spanish nominal lemmas increases the coverage of common nouns by more than 11% (see Tab. 1).

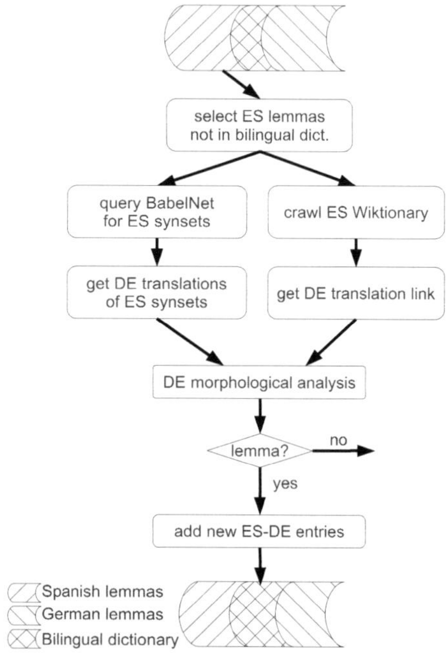


Figure 3: Compilation workflow

| es-de.dix | **end 2013** | **+ new** | **current** |
|---|---|---|---|
| | *Spanish-German entries* | | |
| noun | 16,136 | 7,149 | 23,285 |
| verb | 4,256 | | 4,256 |
| adverb | 316 | | 316 |
| adjective | 5,196 | 640 | 5,836 |
| Total | 25,904 | | **33,693** |
| | *Unique Spanish lemmas* | | |
| noun | 10,559 | 5,528 | 16,087 |
| adjective | 3,029 | 627 | 3,656 |

Table 1: Size of the Spanish-German dictionary at the end of 2013 and after adding entries extracted from BabelNet.

Starting with the vocabulary extracted from a corpus of European Spanish newspaper texts, we expect our bilingual dictionary to be biased with respect to the language variety, register and genre. In our MT project we focus on Peruvian Spanish. Therefore, we want to measure the specific lexical coverage for this variety. In a first step, we compared our Spanish-Quechua dictionary with the Spanish-German lexicon by computing the overlap of their Spanish vocabularies. Only 50% of the 2215 single Spanish verbs with a Quechua translation also have a German equivalent. Crawling Wiktionary for the untranslated 1115 Spanish verbs, we obtained 33 new German verbs. This results in a recall of under 3%, which shows the limit of the method.

In a next step, we measured the overlap for the nouns[5] before and after harvesting the BabelNet translations: the 594 newly covered nouns represent an increase of 8%. The following examples of missing word equivalences show that we can manually find their German translations: *abigeo* (de: Viehdieb; en: rustler, cattle thief), *zapallo* (de: Kürbis; en: pumpkin). However, we want to translate as many of these words as possible automatically into German. Looking at the failures, we observe a large number of participles and adjectives analyzed as common nouns. In a next step, we need to loosen the part-of-speech restriction we have imposed on the filtering.

### 3.5 Corpus coverage

We have collected articles from an online newspaper[6] in order to test the coverage on a Peruvian corpus. This small ad hoc corpus contains about

[5]Note that the "noun" entries in the Spanish-Quechua dictionary also cover Spanish adjectives as there is no morphological distinction between nouns and adjectives in Quechua.

[6]`http://diariodelcusco.com`

10,000 words. In the near future, we will gather more articles and periodically measure the coverage of the growing collection. For the evaluation, we let the MT system do a raw translation (lexical transfer) without lexical disambiguation. Before the extension of the dictionary, the "out-of-vocabulary" ratio of common nouns was 11.95% for tokens and 16.66% for types. With the additional entries extracted from BabelNet, OOV ratios decreased to 7.39% and 11.16%, respectively. Note that the unknown types not only contain single lemmas but also multiword expressions that are not yet listed in the bilingual dictionary.

Applying the same procedure as described in section 3.4, we have added 640 new entries for adjectives to our dictionary. As a result, the OOV ratios of adjective types have decreased from 41.62% to 37.03%. Although the corpus coverage for adjectives improved, it is still low, partly due to the fact that we have not yet treated the participles as adjectives. For example, our dictionary does not have adjective entries for common verb participles like *acompañado* (en: accompanied). Other examples of untranslated adjectives are some toponyms like *limeño* (from Lima), missing from our bilingual dictionary, and *cusqueño* (from Cuzco), absent even from the Spanish full form lexicon. Some common adjective pairs might not be found in BabelNet, e.g. *virtual - virtuell*, but are present in the Wiktionary, and vice versa. For this reason, we combined all possible sources in order to maximize the automatic extension of our dictionary.

## 4 German morphology features

Apart from extending the dictionary with new entries, we added the missing parts of the morphological information needed for the translation from Spanish to German.

### 4.1 German noun gender

For German nouns, in addition to the lemmas, we need at least the gender. In fact, the minimum information depends on the morphological tool we use to generate the German forms.[7] Due to the German agreement constraints, we need the gender of a noun in order to generate the correct inflections on the elements of the noun phrase.[8] Gender information is unequally present in the different sources we have exploited: Almost all the entries retrieved from the "Ding" lexicon and the Wiktionary pages contain the gender of the noun, but BabelNet does not indicate this information.

We applied the same morphology tool (Clematide, 2008) used for generation to analyze the German side of the –with respect to the gender– underspecified dictionary entries. We extracted the analyses with more than one possible gender and manually checked whether the selected gender corresponded to the intended meaning of the Spanish-German lemma pair. We observe different kind of ambiguities: There are true gender alternatives, e.g. *der/das Hektar* is both masculine and neuter, but also homographs with different senses: *die Flur* (en: acre) vs *der Flur* (en: hall). Variable word segmentation within compounds leads to another type of gender ambiguities: the feminine derivative *die Wahrsagerei* (en: fortune telling) is more probable than the neuter compound *das Wahrsager-Ei* (en: the fortune teller's egg).

Automatic gender attribution through morphological analysis is error-prone and far from complete. Nearly a third of the candidate entries extracted from BabelNet received an analysis. We have manually annotated 5% of those entries to roughly estimate the a posteriori precision: 78.5% are correct, 16% wrong, and about 5.5% unclear.

Finally, we need to include the linguistic gender alternation paradigm to gentry nouns and professions. For example, the Spanish word *periodista* refers to both the male and female journalists, but German distinguishes between *Journalist* (masc.) and *Journalistin* (fem.).

### 4.2 German verb auxiliary

German verbs typically use only one of the two auxiliary verbs –*haben* or *sein*– to form the perfect tenses. Nevertheless, some verbs may alternatively use one or the other, depending on the context. Reflexive verbs never use the auxiliary *sein* nor do verbs with a direct object. The most common verb type that requires *sein* as auxiliary are motion verbs, such as *fahren* (en: drive). But if the same verb[9] has a direct object, the auxiliary *haben* appears in the perfect tense form.

[7] This would also be necessary for Spanish, but we are translating only in one direction, from Spanish to German.

[8] Note that German adjectives are inflected according to the gender of the head noun, e.g. in accusative case *'die **grosse** Frau'* (the tall woman) vs *'den **grossen** Mann* (the tall man).

[9] The same surface form may have different verb subcategorization frames.

*sein*: *Ich bin von A nach B gefahren.*

(1) *Ich* **bin** *von A nach B gefahren.*
I **am** from A to B driven.
"I drove from A to B."

*haben*: *Ich habe [mein Auto]$_{DirObj}$ von A nach B gefahren.*

(2) *Ich* **habe** *mein Auto von A nach B gefahren.*
I **have** my car from A to B driven.
"I drove my car from A to B."

Where do we get this information from and how should we best encode this alternative behavior in our dictionary? Unfortunately we cannot automatically get the auxiliaries for every German verb from Canoo, so we extracted 4056 verbs from the Wiktionary dump made available by Henrich et al. (2011). Furthermore, we collected 5465 pages by crawling the Wiktionary for German verbs[10]. As Tab. 2 shows, there are more verbs with auxiliary *haben* than with *sein*, therefore we choose the auxiliary *haben* to be the default. We filtered the verbs with *sein* from both sources and merged them, which resulted in a list of 394 verbs[11].

| Source | verbs | auxiliaries | | |
|---|---|---|---|---|
| | | haben | sein | both |
| dump2011 | 4056 | 3721 | 293 | 17 |
| crawl2013 | 5469 | 4814 | 351 | 200 |
| merged | | | 394 | |

Table 2: Auxiliary verb distribution

The header of our dictionary contains a specific paradigm for the verb entries for which the German translation has to be generated with *sein* in the perfect tenses. This is a derivative version of the default verb paradigm, as Fig. 4 shows.

To select the correct auxiliary we need the syntactic analysis of the German verb phrase or at least the information about the presence or absence of a direct object. If the parse tree obtained from the analysis of the Spanish source sentence is erroneous, we must rely on other means to disambiguate the verb auxiliaries. Which methods are best suited to solve this task is a topic for future work.

[10]`http://de.wiktionary.org/w/index.php?title=Kategorie:Verb_(Deutsch)` [retrieved 2013-12-27]

[11]43 verbs are only in dump2011, 101 only in crawl2013, 250 in both lists.

```
<pardef n="VM_VV_MAIN_BE">
 <e>
  <p>
   <l><s n="parol"/>VM</l>
   <r><s n="aux"/>sein<s n="pos"/>VV</r>
  </p>
  <par n="Verb"/>
 </e>
</pardef>
```

Figure 4: Paradigm definition (`<pardef>`) for main verb pairs (es:`VM`–de:`VV`) with explicit value *sein* for the auxiliary attribute (`aux`) on the German side (`<r>`).

## 5 Conclusion

In our hybrid MT system with a rule-based kernel, the bilingual dictionary plays a crucial role. We have built a Spanish-German dictionary from different freely available resources with general MT in mind. This dictionary contains around 33,700 entries at the moment of writing.[12]

This paper describes the extraction of new entries from BabelNet and Wiktionary. We have shown that these sources can both contribute to the enhancement of our dictionary, albeit on different scales and in a complementary manner. Encouraged by the coverage boost yielded from the addition of nouns and adjectives extracted from BabelNet, we want to apply a similar procedure to verbs. We will also crawl the Wiktionary for the Spanish adjectives and their German equivalents, and continue to gather more information from the net as it gets available. Word derivation is another issue that we want to address, mainly to cover adverbs with the suffix *-mente*, and also to include even more adjectives.

## Acknowledgments

The author would like to thank Annette Rios for her helpful advise and for proof-reading the final version of this paper. This work is funded by the Swiss Nation Science Foundation under grant 100015_132219/1.

[12]Available from our project's website: `http://tiny.uzh.ch/2Q`

## References


Bogdan Babych, Kurt Eberle, Johanna Geiß, Mireia Ginestí-Rosell, Anthony Hartley, Reinhard Rapp, Serge Sharoff, and Martin Thomas. 2012. Design of a hybrid high quality machine translation system. In *Proceedings of the Joint Workshop on Exploiting Synergies between Information Retrieval and Machine Translation (ESIRMT) and Hybrid Approaches to Machine Translation (HyTra)*, pages 101–112, Avignon, France, April. Association for Computational Linguistics.

Sabine Brants, Stefanie Dipper, Peter Eisenberg, Silvia Hansen-Schirra, Esther König, Wolfgang Lezius, Christian Rohrer, George Smith, and Hans Uszkoreit. 2004. TIGER: Linguistic interpretation of a German corpus. *Research on Language and Computation*, 2(4):597–620.

Nicoletta Calzolari, Khalid Choukri, Thierry Declerck, Mehmet Uğur Doğan, Bente Maegaard, Joseph Mariani, Jan Odijk, and Stelios Piperidis, editors. 2012. *Proceedings of the Eight International Conference on Language Resources and Evaluation (LREC'12)*, Istanbul, Turkey, May. European Language Resources Association (ELRA).

Simon Clematide. 2008. An OLIF-based open inflectional resource and yet another morphological system for German. In A. Storrer, A. Geyken, A. Siebert, and K. M. Würzner, editors, *Text Resources and Lexical Knowledge*, number 8 in Text, Translation, Computational Processing, pages 183–194. Mouton de Gruyter, Berlin, Germany, September. KONVENS 2008: Selected Papers from the 9th Conference on Natural Language Processing.

Andreas Eisele and Yu Chen. 2010. MultiUN: A Multilingual Corpus from United Nation Documents. In Daniel Tapias, Mike Rosner, Stelios Piperidis, Jan Odjik, Joseph Mariani, Bente Maegaard, Khalid Choukri, and Nicoletta Calzolari (Conference Chair), editors, *Proceedings of the Seventh Conference on International Language Resources and Evaluation*, pages 2868–2872. European Language Resources Association (ELRA), May.

Carla Parra Escartín. 2012. Design and compilation of a specialized Spanish-German parallel corpus. In Calzolari et al. (Calzolari et al., 2012).

Aitor Gonzalez-Agirre, Egoitz Laparra, and German Rigau. 2012. Multilingual Central Repository version 3.0: upgrading a very large lexical knowledge base. In *Proceedings of the Sixth International Global WordNet Conference (GWC'12)*, Matsue, Japan.

Verena Henrich, Erhard Hinrichs, and Tatiana Vodolazova. 2011. Semi-Automatic Extension of GermaNet with Sense Definitions from Wiktionary. In *Proceedings of the 5th Language & Technology Conference (LTC 2011)*, pages 126–130, Pozna, Poland, November.

Philipp Koehn. 2005. Europarl: a parallel corpus for statistical machine translation. In *Proceedings of the 10th MT Summit*, pages 79–86, Phuket, Thailand, September. European Association for Machine Translation.

Montserrat Marimon, Natalia Seghezzi, and Núria Bel. 2007. An Open-source Lexicon for Spanish. *Procesamiento del Lenguaje Natural*, 39:131–137.

Aingeru Mayor, Iñaki Alegria, Arantza Díaz de Ilarraza, Gorka Labaka, Mikel Lersundi, and Kepa Sarasola. 2012. Matxin, an open-source rule-based machine translation system for Basque. *Machine Translation*, (25):53–82.

Ryan McDonald, Joakim Nivre, Yvonne Quirmbach-Brundage, Yoav Goldberg, Dipanjan Das, Kuzman Ganchev, Keith Hall, Slav Petrov, Hao Zhang, Oscar Täckström, Claudia Bedini, Núria Bertomeu Castelló, and Jungmee Lee. 2013. Universal Dependency Annotation for Multilingual Parsing. In *Proceedings of the 51st Annual Meeting of the Association for Computational Linguistics (Volume 2: Short Papers)*, pages 92–97, Sofia, Bulgaria, August. Association for Computational Linguistics.

Roberto Navigli and Simone Paolo Ponzetto. 2012. BabelNet: The Automatic Construction, Evaluation and Application of a Wide-Coverage Multilingual Semantic Network. *Artificial Intelligence*, 193:217–250.

Lluís Padró and Evgeny Stanilovsky. 2012. FreeLing 3.0: Towards Wider Multilinguality. In Calzolari et al. (Calzolari et al., 2012).

Annette Rios and Anne Göhring. 2012. A tree is a Baum is an árbol is a sach'a: Creating a trilingual treebank. In Calzolari et al. (Calzolari et al., 2012), pages 1874–1879.

Mariona Taulé, M. Antònia Martí, and Marta Recasens. 2008. AnCora: Multilevel Annotated Corpora for Catalan and Spanish. In Nicoletta Calzolari, Khalid Choukri, Bente Maegaard, Joseph Mariani, Jan Odijk, Stelios Piperidis, and Daniel Tapias, editors, *Proceedings of the Sixth International Language Resources and Evaluation (LREC'08)*, Marrakech, Marroco.

Špela Vintar, Darja Fišer, and Aljoša Vrščaj. 2012. Were the clocks striking or surprising? Using WSD to improve MT performance. In *Proceedings of the Joint Workshop on Exploiting Synergies between Information Retrieval and Machine Translation (ESIRMT) and Hybrid Approaches to Machine Translation (HyTra)*, pages 87–92, Avignon, France, April. Association for Computational Linguistics.

# An Empirical Study of the Impact of Idioms on Phrase Based Statistical Machine Translation of English to Brazilian-Portuguese

**Giancarlo D. Salton** and **Robert J. Ross** and **John D. Kelleher**
Applied Intelligence Research Centre
School of Computing
Dublin Institute of Technology
Ireland
giancarlo.salton@mydit.ie {robert.ross,john.d.kelleher}@dit.ie

### Abstract

This paper describes an experiment to evaluate the impact of idioms on Statistical Machine Translation (SMT) process using the language pair English/Brazilian-Portuguese. Our results show that on sentences containing idioms a standard SMT system achieves about half the BLEU score of the same system when applied to sentences that do not contain idioms. We also provide a short error analysis and outline our planned work to overcome this limitation.

## 1 Introduction and Motivation

An idiom is an expression whose meaning is not compositional (Xatara, 2001). In other words the meaning of an idiom is not simply the joint meaning of the individual words (Garrao and Dias, 2001). For example, the expression *kick the bucket* has an idiomatic meaning (*to die*) that has nothing to do with the meaning of *kick* or *bucket*.

Idioms are a type of multi-word expressions (MWEs) often used in a large variety of texts and by human speakers and thus appear in all languages (Fazly et al., 2008). Consequently, they pose problems to most Natural Language Processing (NLP) applications (Sag et al., 2002). Nevertheless, they often have been overlooked by researchers in NLP (Fazly et al., 2008).

As a class, idioms exhibit a number of properties that make them difficult to handle for NLP applications. For example, idiomatic expressions vary with respect to how morphosyntatically fixed they are. An idiomatic expression is highly fixed if the replacement of any of its constituents by a, syntactically or semantically, similar word causes the idiomatic meaning of the expression to be lost (Fazly et al., 2008). An example of a highly fixed idiom in English is the expression *by and large*. Idioms that are highly fixed can be represented as words-with-spaces by an NLP system (Sag et al., 2002). If, however, an idiomatic meaning persists across morphosyntactic variations of an expression, the idiom can be described as a low fixed idiom, for example, *hold fire* and its variations *hold one's fire* and *held fire*. The words-with-spaces approach does not work for these "more flexible" example of idioms (Fazly et al., 2008). Another feature of idioms that make them difficult for NLP system to process is that idiomatic expressions have both idiomatic and literal (non-idiomatic) usages. Consequently, NLP systems need to distinguish between these types of usages (Fazly et al., 2008).

One of the most important NLP applications that is negatively affected by idioms is Statistical Machine Translation (SMT) systems. The current state-of-the-art in SMT are phrase-based systems (Collins et al., 2005). Phrase-based SMT systems extend the basic SMT word-by-word approach by splitting the translation process into 3 steps: the input source sentence is segmented into "phrases" or multi-word units; these phrases are translated into the target language; and the translated phrases are reordered if needed (Koehn, 2010).

It is worth highlighting that although the term phrase-based translation seems to imply the system works at a phrasal level, the concept of a phrase to these systems is simply a frequently occurring sequence of words and not necessarily a semantic or grammatical phrase. These systems thus limit themselves to a direct translation of phrases without any syntactic or semantic context. Hence, standard phrase-based SMT systems do not model idioms explicitly (Bouamor et al., 2011). Unfortunately modelling idioms in order to improve SMT is not well studied (Ren et al., 2009) and examples of the difficulties in translating these expressions can be seen in the quality of the resultant output of most Machine Translation systems (Vieira and Lima, 2001).

Our long-term research goal is to investigate how the translation of idiomatic expressions may be improved. We will initially focus on the case of English/Brazillian-Portugese but we intend our work to be generalizable to other language pairs. As a first step on this research program we wished to scope the impact of idioms on an SMT system. In order to test this we ran an experiment that compared the BLEU scores of an SMT system when it was tested on three distinct sentence aligned corpora. Two of these test corpora consisted of sentences containing idiomatic (rather than literal) usages of idiomatic expressions and the other corpus consisted of sentences that did not contain any idioms. By comparing the BLEU score of a machine translation system on each of these corpora we hoped to gauge the size of the research problem we are addressing.

The paper is organized as follows: Section 2 describes the design and creation of the corpora used in the experiments; Section 3 presents the experiment's methodology; Section 4 reports the results found; and Section 5 both discusses the results and describes an approach to the problem that we will implement in future work.

## 2 Related work

The work of Fazly et al. (2008) has provided an inspirational basis for our work. Fazly's work focused on the study of idioms and in particular their identification and analysis in terms of the syntactic and semantic fixedness. Fazly study did not however explore the impact of idioms on SMT.

Some related work in translating idioms can be found in: Garrao and Dias (2001) where the verb+noun combinations and their inclusion in an online automatic translator is explored; Ren et al. (2009) which makes use of a domain constrained bilingual multi-word dictionary to improve the MT results; Bouamor et al. (2011) which explores a hybrid approach for extracting MWEs and their translation in a French-English corpus; and Bungum et al. (2013) which also uses dictionaries to capture MWEs.

None of these works compares the BLEU score of sentences containing and not containing idioms. And also, none of these works address the idioms problem for the English/Brazilian-Portuguese language pair using SMT phrase-based systems.

## 3 Corpora Design and Collection

The experiment we describe in this paper had two direct targets: (a) we wished to quantify the effect of idioms on the performance of an SMT system; and (b) we wanted to better understand the differences (if any) between high and low fixed idioms with respect to their impact on SMT systems. Consequently, in order to run the experiments four corpora were needed: one initial large sentence-aligned bilingual corpus was needed to build an SMT model for the language pair English/Brazilian-Portuguese; a test corpus containing sentences with "highly fixed" idioms called the "High Idiomatic Corpus"; another test corpus containing sentences with "low fixed" idioms called the "Low Idiomatic Corpus"; and a last corpus with sentences not containing idioms called the "Clean Corpus". In order to make the results comparable the length of each sentence in the three test corpora was kept between 15 to 20 words. All of these corpora were constructed by hand and in the cases of the "High Idiomatic Corpus" and "Low Idiomatic Corpus" care was taken to ensure that all the sentences in these corpora contained idiomatic usages of the relevant idioms.

To create the initial large corpus a series of small corpora available on the internet were compiled into one larger corpus which was used to train a SMT system. The resources used in this step were the Fapesp-v2 (Aziz and Specia, 2011), the OpenSubtitles2013[1] corpus, the PHP Manual Corpus[2] and the KDE4 localizaton files (v.2)[3]. No special tool was used to clean these corpora and the files were compiled as is.

Idioms are a heterogeneous class; consequently, in order to better control the experiment we decided to focus on a particular type of idiom - specifically the idiomatic expressions formed from the combination of a verb and a noun as its direct object (verb+noun combinations), for example *hit+road* and *lose+head*. Verb+noun combinations are a subclass of MWE which are notable for their cross-lingual occurrence and high variability, both lexical and semantic (Baldwin and Kim, 2010). Also, it is worth noting that it is possible for a particular verb+noun combination to have both idiomatic and literal usages and these usages must be distinguished if an NLP system is to pro-

[1]http://opus.lingfil.uu.se/OpenSubtitles2013.php

[2]http://opus.lingfil.uu.se/PHP.php

[3]http://opus.lingfil.uu.se/KDE4.php

cess a sentence appropriately.

Fazly et al. (2008) named a dataset of 17 "highly fixed" English verb+noun idioms, for example *cut+figure*, and that list was used to build our "Highly Idiomatic Corpus". This corpus consisted of 170 sentences containing idiomatic usages of these idioms, 10 sentences per idiom in the list. These English sentences were collected from the internet and manually translated into Brazilian-Portuguese. After that these translations were then manually checked and corrected by a second translator.

Fazly et al. (2008) also named a dataset of 11 "low fixed" English verb+noun idioms, for example *get+wind*, and that list was used to build our "Low Idiomatic Corpus". This corpus consisted of 110 sentences containing idiomatic usages of these idioms, 10 sentences per idiom in the list. These English sentences were also collected from the internet and manually translated into Brazilian-Portuguese. After this step these translations were also manually checked and corrected by a second translator. Table 1 presents the English verb+noun combinations used in this experiment and their Brazilian-Portuguese translations.

In order to have a valid comparison between the translation results of sentences containing and not containing idioms the "Clean Corpus" was built. It consisted of 850 sentences with their translations and was created by sampling sentences of the appropriate length (15-20 words) that did not contain idioms from the large bilingual corpus (that we described earlier) which we created to train the SMT system. These sentences were then removed from that corpus. Because the initial corpus was created from the union of corpora from different domains the "Clean Corpus" was randomly split into 5 datasets containing 170 sentences each in order to ensure no specific influence of any of those domains on the BLEU score. We called these "Clean1" to "Clean5". Special care was taken to not have any idioms in any of the sentences in these corpora.

As we wanted to collect 10 sentences for each verb+noun idiomatic combination and due to the limitations of sentence length (15 to 20 words) we were not able to collect the "High Idiomatic Corpus" and the "Low Idiomatic Corpus" from the training corpus. Thus, the samples were collected from the Internet.

## 4 Methodology

As a first step for this experiment, a SMT model for the English/Brazilian-Portuguese language pair was trained using the Moses toolkit (Koehn et al., 2007) following its "baseline" settings (Koehn et al., 2008). The corpus used for this training consisted of 17,288,109 pairs of sentences (approximately 50% of the initial collected corpus), with another 34,576 pairs of sentences used for the "tuning" process.

| **English** | **Brazilian-Portuguese** |
|---|---|
| blow+top | perder+paciência |
| blow+trumpet | *"gabar-se"* |
| cut+figure | causar+impressão |
| find+foot | *"adaptar-se"* |
| get+nod | *"obter permissão"* |
| give+sack | *"ser demitido", "demitir"* |
| have+word | ter+conversa |
| hit+road | *"cair na estrada"* |
| hit+roof | *"ficar zangado"* |
| kick+heel | *"deixar esperando"* |
| lose+thread | *"perder o fio da meada"* |
| make+face* | fazer+careta |
| make+mark | deixar+marca |
| pull+plug | *"cancelar algo"* |
| pull+punch | *"esconder algo"* |
| pull+weight | *"fazer sua parte"* |
| take+heart | *"ficar confiante"* |
| blow+whistle | *"botar a boca no trombone"'* |
| get+wind | ouvir+murmúrios |
| hit+wall | *"dar de cara num muro"* |
| hold+fire | *"conter-se"* |
| lose+head* | perder+cabeça |
| make+hay | dar+graças |
| make+hit | fazer+sucesso |
| make+pile | fazer+grana |
| make+scene* | fazer+cena |
| pull+leg | pegar+pé |
| see+star* | ver+estrela |

Table 1: The English verb+noun combinations used in this experiment and their Brazilian-Portuguese Translations. The idioms marked with an * have direct translations of its constituents resulting in a MWE with the same idiomatic meaning in Brazilian-Portuguese. Also, note that not all translations results in a verb+noun idiom in the target language. Those are presented between double quotes and italics.

In the second step the BLEU scores for the "High Idiomatic Corpus", the "Low Idiomatic Corpus" and the five clean corpora were computed. Then, the average of each evaluation for the clean corpora was calculated.

## 5 Results and Analysis

Table 2 lists the SMT system BLEU scores for the "High Idiomatic Corpus", "Low Idiomatic Corpus", and the average BLEU score for the clean corpora (i.e, "Clean1" to "Clean5"). The differential between the BLEU scores for the clean corpus and the idiomatic corpora (high and low) indicates that English idiomatic expressions of the verb+noun type pose a significant challenge to standard phrase based SMT.

| Corpus | BLEU scores |
|---|---|
| High Idiomatic | 23.12 |
| Low Idiomatic | 24.55 |
| Clean (average) | 46.28 |

Table 2: BLEU scores.

The corpora containing idioms achieved only half of the average Clean Corpus score. As noted earlier, some idioms have a direct translation from English to Brazilian-Portuguese and could result in straight forward translations that the basic SMT system (without substitution) can handle correctly. Given this, the BLEU scores for this subset of idioms could be expected to be similar to the clean corpus results. However, it is worth noting that even for idioms that have direct translations, see Table 1, the BLEU score for the sentences containing these idioms is still lower than average BLEU score for the clean corpus. Using the Student's $t$-test, we found a statistical difference between the "Low Idiomatic Corpus" and the "Clean Corpus" ($p \ll 0$), and between the "High Idiomatic Corpus" and the "Clean Corpus" ($p \ll 0$).

The second question that we examined in the experiment was whether there was a difference in performance between the high and low fixed idioms. Table 3 lists the BLEU scores for each of the "highly fixed" verb+noun combinations used in the "High Idiomatic Corpus" and Table 4 lists the BLEU scores for each of the "low fixed" verb+noun combinations from the "Low Idiomatic Corpus". Also, it is important to note that the "High Idiomatic Corpus" and the "Low Idiomatic Corpus" have almost no difference in their BLEU scores. We also found that there are almost no statistical difference ($p = 0.85$) between the "High Idiomatic Corpus" and "Low Idiomatic Corpus" which we believe indicates that both kinds of verb+noun idiomatic combinations pose the same problem to SMT.

| "high fixed" verb+noun | BLEU score |
|---|---|
| *blow+top* | 22.08 |
| *blow+trumpet* | 19.38 |
| *cut+figure* | 20.15 |
| *find+foot* | 24.36 |
| *get+nod* | 22.06 |
| *give+sack* | 23.03 |
| *have+word* | 20.91 |
| *hit+road* | 24.53 |
| *hit+roof* | 21.34 |
| *kick+heel* | 18.85 |
| *lose+thread* | 21.81 |
| *make+face* | 28.62 |
| *make+mark* | 29.46 |
| *pull+plug* | 19.71 |
| *pull+punch* | 28.34 |
| *pull+weight* | 19.94 |
| *take+heart* | 23.41 |

Table 3: BLEU scores for individual "high fixed" verb+noun idiomatic combinations.

| "low fixed" verb+noun | BLEU score |
|---|---|
| *blow+whistle* | 17.75 |
| *get+wind* | 19.06 |
| *hit+wall* | 16.52 |
| *hold+fire* | 23.26 |
| *lose+head* | 37.40 |
| *make+hay* | 15.87 |
| *make+hit* | 25.48 |
| *make+pile* | 25.31 |
| *make+scene* | 36.93 |
| *pull+leg* | 15.90 |
| *see+star* | 37.86 |

Table 4: BLEU scores for individual "low fixed" verb+noun idiomatic combinations.

## 6 Conclusions and Future Work

Certainly, these results are not surprising. BLEU scores are generally dependent on the training and test corpora; that said, it it worthwhile having a quantification of the potential issues that idioms pose for SMT. Due to the fact that BLEU scores are dependent on the training and test corpora used our results are corpus specific. However, these results are our starting point to develop a hybrid methodology.

As noted earlier, idioms are widely used in every literary genre and new expressions come into existence frequently. Thus, they must be properly handled and translated by a Machine Translation system. Given the results of our experiments it is evident that the problem in translating idioms has not been solved using a standard SMT system. Such evidences and the relatively small amount of current related work on idiomatic expression translation, when compared with the amount of work on other MT aspects, indicates that there is likely not a trivial solution.

To start addressing these problems, we propose a hybrid method inspired by the work developed by Okuma et al. (2008) for translating unseen words using bilingual dictionaries.

Our method, introduced in Salton et al. (2014), work as a pre and post-processing step. We first identify idioms in source sentences using an idiom dictionary. Then, we substitute the idiom in the source sentence with its literal meaning, taken from the dictionary and record the fact that this sentence contained a substituted idiom. For all sentences that are recorded as containing a substitution, after the translation we check if the original idiom that occurred in the source sentence has a corresponding idiom in the target language by consulting a separate bilingual dictionary. If there is a corresponding idiom in the target language then the translation of the literal meaning of the source language idiom is replaced with the target language idiom. If there are no related idioms on the target language, this post-processing step is avoided and the translation is done.

This approach relies on a number of dictionaries being available. Developing these resources is non-trivial and in order to scale our approach to broad coverage a large part of our future work will focus on automating (as much as possible) the development of these language resources. Another problem that we will address in future work is ensuring that we apply substitution appropriately. There are at least two situations where care must be taken. First, a given expression may be used both as an idiom and literally. Consequently, we need to develop mechanisms that will enable our preprocessing step to distinguish between idiomatic and non-idiomatic usages. Second, some idiomatic expressions have direct translations. For these expressions we expect that the substitution method may under-perform the standard SMT system. Ideally, we would like to be able to control the substitution method so that these particular expressions are allowed through the preprocessing and are handled by the standard SMT pipeline. However, for now, considering the proportion of expressions with direct translations in comparison with the overall number of expressions is very low; we hope that this problem will not have too adverse an impact on our approach. Beyond these issues, while we anticipate that our substitution based approached will work reasonably well for "high fixed" idioms, we are aware that the variation in "low fixed" idioms may require us to extend the system in order to handle this variation.

## Acknowledgments

Giancarlo D. Salton would like to thank CAPES ("Coordenação de Aperfeiçoamento de Pessoal de Nível Superior") for his Science Without Borders scholarship, proc n. 9050-13-2. We would like to thank Acassia Thabata de Souza Salton for her corrections on the Brazilian-Portuguese translation of sentences containing idioms.

## References

Wilker Aziz and Lucia Specia. 2011. Fully automatic compilation of a portuguese-english and portuguese-spanish parallel corpus for statistical machine translation. In *STIL 2011*.

Timothy Baldwin and Su Nam Kim. 2010. Multiword Expressions. In Nitin Indurkhya and Fred J. Damerau, editors, *Handbook of Natural Language Processing, Second Edition*. CRC Press, Taylor and Francis Group.

Dhouha Bouamor, Nasredine Semmar, and Pierre Zweigenbaum. 2011. Improved Statistical Machine Translation Using MultiWord Expressions. In *Proceedings of the International Workshop on Using Linguistic Information for Hybrid Machine Translation)*, pages 15–20.

Lars Bungum, Björn Gambäck, André Lynum, and Erwin Marsi. 2013. Improving Word Translation Disambiguation by Capturing Multiword Expressions with Dictionaries. In *Proceedings of the 9th Workshop on Multiword Expressions (MWE 2013)*, pages 21–30.

Michael Collins, Philipp Koehn, and Ivona Kučerová. 2005. Clause Restructuring for Statistical Machine

Translation. In *Proceedings of the 43rd Annual Meeting of the ACL*, pages 531–540.

Afsaneh Fazly, Paul Cook, and Suzanne Stevenson. 2008. Unsupervised Type and Token Identification of Idiomatic Expressions. In *Computational Linguistics*, volume 35, pages 61–103.

Milena U. Garrao and Maria C. P. Dias. 2001. Um Estudo de Expressões Cristalizadas do Tipo V+Sn e sua Inclusão em um Tradutor Automático Bilíngüe (Português/Inglês). In *Cadernos de Tradução*, volume 2, pages 165–182.

Philipp Koehn, Hieu Hoang, Alexandra Birch, Chris Callison-Burch, Marcello Federico, Nicola Bertoldi, Brooke Cowan, Wade Shen, Christine Moran, Richard Zens, Chris Dyer, Ondrej Bojar, Alexandra Constantin, and Evan Herbst. 2007. Moses: Open Source Toolkit for Statistical Machine Translation. In *45th Annual Meeting of the Association for Computational Linguistics*.

Philipp Koehn, Abhishek Arun, and Hieu Hoang. 2008. Towards better machine translation quality for the German-English language pairs. In *Proceedings of the Third Workshop on Statistical Machine Translation*, pages 139–142.

Philipp Koehn. 2010. *Statistical Machine Translation*. Cambridge University Press, New York. 2 Ed.

Hideo Okuma, Hirofumi Yamamoto, and Eiichiro Sumita. 2008. Introducing Translation Dictionary Into Phrase-based SMT. In *IEICE - Transactions on Information and Systems*, number 7, pages 2051–2057.

Zhixiang Ren, Yajuan Lu, Jie Cao, Qun Liu, and Yun Huang. 2009. Improving statistical machine translation using domain bilingual multiword expressions. In *Proceedings of the 2009 Workshop on Multiword Expressions, ACL-IJCNLP 2009*, pages 47–54.

Ivan A. Sag, Thimothy Baldwin, Francis Bond, Ann Copestake, and Dan Flickinger. 2002. Multiword Expressions: A Pain in the Neck for NLP. In *Computational Linguistics and Intelligent Text Processing: Third International Conference: CICLing-2002, Lecture Notes in Computer Science*, volume 2276, pages 1–15.

Giancarlo D. Salton, Robert J. Ross, and John D. Kelleher. 2014. Evaluation of a Substitution Method for Idiom Transformation in Statistical Machine Translation. In *The 10th Workshop on Multiword Expressions (MWE 2014) at 14th Conference of the European Chapter of the Association for Computational Linguistics*.

Renata Vieira and Vera Lcia S. Lima. 2001. Linguística Computacional: Princípios e aplicações. In *Ana Teresa Martins & Díbio Leandro Borges (eds.), As Tecnologias da informação e a questão social: anais*.

Cláudia M. Xatara. 2001. O Ensino do Léxico: As Expressões Idiomáticas. In *Trabalhos em Linguística Aplicada*, volume 37, pages 49–59.

# Resumptive Pronoun Detection for Modern Standard Arabic to English MT

**Stephen Tratz*** **Clare Voss*** **Jamal Laoudi†**
*Army Research Laboratory, Adelphi, MD 20783
†Advanced Resource Technologies, Inc. Alexandria, VA 22314
{stephen.c.tratz.civ,clare.r.voss.civ,jamal.laoudi.ctr}@mail.mil

## Abstract

Many languages, including Modern Standard Arabic (MSA), insert resumptive pronouns in relative clauses, whereas many others, such as English, do not, using empty categories instead. This discrepancy is a source of difficulty when translating between these languages because there are words in one language that correspond to empty categories in the other, and these words must either be inserted or deleted—depending on translation direction. In this paper, we first examine challenges presented by resumptive pronouns in MSA-English translations and review resumptive pronoun translations generated by a popular online MSA-English MT engine. We then present what is, to the best of our knowledge, the first system for automatic identification of resumptive pronouns. The system achieves 91.9 F1 and 77.8 F1 on Arabic Treebank data when using gold standard parses and automatic parses, respectively.

## 1 Introduction

One of the challenges for modern machine translation (MT) is the need to systematically insert or delete information that is overtly expressed in only one of the languages in order to maintain intelligibility and/or fluency. For example, word alignment between pro-drop and non-pro-drop languages can be negatively impacted by the systematic dropping of pronouns in only one of the languages (Xiang et al., 2013). A similar type of linguistic phenomenon of great interest to linguists that has not yet received significant attention in MT research is the mismatch between languages in their usage of resumptive pronouns. Some languages, such as Modern Standard Arabic (MSA), require the insertion of resumptive pronouns in many relative clauses, whereas other languages, including English, rarely permit them. An example of an MSA sentence is given below, with its English gloss showing the resumptive pronoun in bold, its reference translation (RT), and an MT system output where the roles of *patient* and *doctor* are incorrectly reversed:

رأيت المريض الذي أنقذته الطبيبة

Gloss: *I.saw the.patient who rescued.***him** *the.doctor.*
RT: *I saw the patient whom the doctor rescued.*
MT: *I saw a patient who rescued the doctor.*

In this paper, we examine translations produced by a popular online translation system for MSA resumptive pronouns occurring in several different syntactic positions to gain insight into the types of errors generated by current MT engines. In a test suite of 300 MSA sentences with resumptive pronouns, over 30% of the relative clauses with resumptive pronouns were translated inaccurately. We then present an automatic classifier that we built for identifying MSA resumptive pronouns and the results obtained from using it in experiments with the Arabic Treebank (Maamouri et al., 2004; Maamouri and Bies, 2004). The system achieves 91.9 F1 and 77.8 F1 on Arabic Treebank data when using gold standard parses and automatic parses, respectively. To the best of our knowledge, this is the first attempt to automatically identify resumptive pronouns in any language.

## 2 Relevant MSA Linguistics

MSA and English relative clauses differ in structure, with one of the most prominent differences being in regard to resumptive pronouns. Resumptive pronouns are required in many MSA relative clauses but are almost never grammatical in English. In MSA, like English, if the external

| | Arabic (أعرف...) | Gloss (I know...) | English RT (I know...) | MT Output (I know...) |
|---|---|---|---|---|
| 1a | السيدة التي تبتسم كثيرا | the+lady who$_i$ $\epsilon_i$ smiles a_lot | the lady who$_i$ $\epsilon_i$ smiles a lot | the lady who smiles a lot |
| 1b | سيدة تبتسم كثيرا | lady $\omega_i$ smiles $\epsilon_i$ a_lot | a lady who$_i$ $\epsilon_i$ smiles a lot | a lot lady smiling |
| 1c | من يبتسم كثيرا | who$_i$ smiles $\epsilon_i$ a_lot | who$_i$ $\epsilon_i$ smiles a lot | a lot of smiles |
| 2a | الشركة التي مولها الرجل | the+company that$_i$ financed+it$_i$ the+man | the company that$_i$ the man financed $\epsilon_i$ | the company that financed the man |
| 2b | شركة مولها الرجل | company $\omega_i$ financed+it$_i$ the+man | a company $\omega_i$ the man financed $\epsilon_i$ | a company funded by the man |
| 2c | ما موله الرجل | what$_i$ financed+it$_i$ the+man | what$_i$ the man financed $\epsilon_i$ | what the man-funded |
| 3a | الولد الذي تكلمت الفتاة معه | the+boy whom$_i$ talked the+girl with+him$_i$ | the boy whom$_i$ the girl talked with $\epsilon_i$ | the boy who spoke with the girl |
| 3b | ولدا تكلمت الفتاة معه | boy $\omega_i$ talked the+girl with+him$_i$ | a boy $\omega_i$ the girl talked with $\epsilon_i$ | the girl was born I spoke with him |
| 3c | مع من تكلمت الفتاة | [with whom]$_i$ talked the+girl $\epsilon_i$ | [with whom]$_i$ the girl talked $\epsilon_i$ | from speaking with the girl |
| 4a | الرجل الذي انهار منزله | the+man who$_i$ collapsed house+his$_i$ | the man [whose house]$_i$ $\epsilon_i$ collapsed | a man who collapsed home |
| 4b | رجلا انهار منزله | man $\omega_i$ collapsed house+his$_i$ | a man [whose house]$_i$ $\epsilon_i$ collapsed | a man of his house collapsed |
| 4c | من انهار منزله | who$_i$ collapsed house+his$_i$ | [whose house]$_i$ $\epsilon_i$ collapsed | of his house collapsed |
| 5 | ما هو منطقي | what$_i$ it$_i$ logical | what$_i$ $\epsilon_i$ is logical | what is logical |

Table 1: A list of MSA sentences starting with relative clauses أعرف (translation: I know) along with their English glosses, English reference translation (RT), and the output of MT system X. Empty categories are indicated with $\epsilon$ and empty WH nodes are indicated with $\omega$. Subscripts indicate coreference. To avoid clutter, the glosses do not explicitly indicate person, number, or gender.

antecedent plays the role of the subject, no resumptive pronoun is inserted[1]; instead, MSA inflects the verb to agree with the subject in number and gender by attaching an affix[2]. A second significant difference between the two languages is that, in MSA, relative pronouns are required for relative clauses modifying definite noun phrases but are prohibited when modifying indefinite noun phrases; in English, definitiveness neither prevents nor necessitates the inclusion of a relative pronoun. A third significant difference is that, for free relative clauses—that is, relative clauses that are not attached to an external antecedent—MSA has a different set of relative pronouns for introducing the clause[3]. A fourth challenge is that MSA has no equivalent word for the English word 'whose' and, to convey a similar meaning, employs resumptive pronouns as possessive modifiers. Examples illustrating these differences are provided in Table 1. For further background on MSA relative clauses and MSA grammar, we refer readers to books by Ryding (2005) and Badawi et al. (2004).

[1]A notable exception to this rule is for equational sentences. MSA lacks an overt copula corresponding to the English word 'is' and, to convey a similar meaning, resumptive subject pronouns must be inserted in these contexts.

[2]In standard VSO and VOS constructions, the verbs inflect as singular regardless of the number of the subject.

[3]These pronouns are also employed to introduce questions.

## 3 Data

In our research, we rely on the conversion of constituent into dependency structures and the training/dev/test splits of the Arabic Treebank (ATB) parts 1, 2, & 3 (Maamouri et al., 2004; Maamouri and Bies, 2004) as presented by Tratz (2013). We extract features from labeled dependency trees (rather than constituent trees) generated by Tratz's (2013) Arabic NLP system, which separates clitics, labels parts-of-speech, produces dependency parses, and identifies and labels affixes.

The original ATB dependency conversion does not mark pronouns for resumptiveness, so we modify the conversion process to obtain this information. The original ATB constituent trees mark this by labeling WHNP nodes and NP nodes with identical indices. If the NP node corresponds to a null subject and the head of the S under the SBAR is a verb, we mark the inflectional affix on the verb, which agrees with the subject in gender and number, as resumptive. These inflectional affixes are included as their own category within our analyses since their presence precludes the appearance of another resumptive pronoun within the relative clause (e.g., as a direct object).

The total number of resumptive pronouns and "resumptive" inflectional affixes in the training, dev, and test sections are presented in Table 2. In

| | Training | Dev | Test |
|---|---|---|---|
| Pronouns | 5775 | 794 | 796 |
| Inflectional affixes | 6161 | 807 | 845 |

Table 2: Number of resumptive pronouns and "resumptive" inflectional affixes by data section.

the training data, the four most likely positions[4] for the resumptive pronouns are:

i) direct object of relative clause's main verb (33.9%)

ii) object of a preposition attached to the verb (20.8%)

iii) possessive modifier of the subject of the verb (5.4%)

iv) subject pronoun in an equational sentence (4.2%).

## 4 Translation Error Analysis

As an exploratory exercise to gain insight into the types of errors generated by current MT engines when translating from a language that inserts resumptive pronouns (i.e., MSA) to one that doesn't (i.e., English), we worked with a native Arabic speaker to produce a list of Arabic sentences that vary in terms of definitiveness (and existence, as with free relatives) of the external antecedent, and the syntactic position of the resumptive pronoun, along with English glosses and reference translations for these sentences. This set was then processed using a popular online translation system, which we refer to as system X. The sentences, their glosses, reference translations, and automatic translations are presented in Table 1.

Although system X did not typically produce English pronouns corresponding to the resumptive pronouns in the source, most of the translations proved problematic, with many of the issues being related to reordering. Thus, while system X appears to be good at not translating resumptive pronouns, its performance on the relative clauses that contain them has ample room for improvement. Our working hypothesis is that system X's English language model is effective in discounting candidate translations that keep the resumptive pronoun.

As a second exploratory exercise, we automatically extracted all the resumptive pronoun examples in the training section of the data described in Section 3 and grouped them based upon the sequence of dependency arc labels from the resumptive pronoun up to the head of the relative clause and the first letter of the POS tag of the intervening words (e.g., 'N' for noun, 'A' for adjective). For each of the thirty most common configurations, we took ten examples (for a total of 300), ran them through system X's Arabic-English model and gave both the translation and the source text to our native Arabic expert. Our expert examined whether 1) the translation engine generated a pronoun corresponding to the source side resumptive pronoun and 2) whether the translation was correct locally within the relative clause (whether the pronoun was retained or not)[5]. The results for these two judgments are presented in Table 3.

| | | Corresponding Pronoun? | |
|---|---|---|---|
| | | Yes | No |
| Correct? | Yes | 17 | 189 |
| | No | 20 | 74 |

Table 3: Expert judgments

Our expert concluded that a corresponding English pronoun was produced in only 37 of the 300 examples (12.3%). Seventeen of these were judged correct, although in many of these cases a significant portion of the relative clause was translated incorrectly even though a small portion including the pronoun was translated properly, making judgment difficult. Our expert noted that many of the correct translations involved switching the voice of the verb in the relative clause from active to passive voice using a past participle. Of the 189 that had no corresponding pronoun and were judged correct, 46 (24.3%) involved switching to passive voice. In general, it appears that system X does a good job at not generating English pronouns corresponding to MSA resumptive pronouns, although it makes numerous mistakes with the data we presented to it.

## 5 System Description

Our MSA resumptive pronoun identification system processes one sentence at a time and relies upon the (averaged) structured perceptron algorithm (Collins, 2002) to rank the feasible actions. When processing a sentence containing $n$ pronouns and affixes, a total of $n$ iterations are performed. During each processing iteration, the system considers two actions for every unlabeled

[4]Examples of these frequent configurations are in Table 1.

[5]This latter task was challenging, but permitted, as intended, lenient judgment of the MT output.

**Function Definitions:**
*path*(x) – returns a list of dependency arcs from x up through the first 'ripcmp', 'rcmod', or 'ROOT' arc (link from affix to the core word is also treated as an arc)
*rDescendants*(x) – returns a list of paths (dependency arc lists) from x to each descendant already marked as resumptive
*pDescendants*(x) – returns a list of paths (dependency arc lists) from x to each pronoun / verbal inflectional affix, not following 'cc', 'ripcmp', or 'rcmod' arcs
*hasDepArc*(x,y) – returns a Boolean value indicating if an arc with label y descends from x
*pathToString*(x) – concatenates the labels of the arcs in a list to create a string
*last*(x) – returns the last element in the list x
*split*(x, y) – splits a string x apart wherever it contains substring y, returning these pieces
*deps(x)*, *parent(x)* – return dependency arc(s) of which x is the {head, child}
*head(x)*, *child(x)* – returns the {head, child} of arc x
*pro(x)* – if x is an affix, the word attached to it is returned, otherwise x is returned
*l(x)* – return the label/part-of-speech for a dependency arc, affix, or word
*T(x)*, *t(x)*, *suffixes(x)* – return the {type ('affix' or 'pro'), written text, suffixes} for x
*n(x,y)* – returns the word node that is y words after *pro(x)*

**Given:** p – pronoun or inflectional affix

**Pseudocode:**
```
'0:'+T(p), '1:'+t(p), '2:'+l(p), '3:'+l(parent(p)), for(s in split(l(p),'_')) { '4:'+s }
if(T(p)='affix') { for(a in deps(pro(p))) { '5:'+l(a) }, if(T(p)='pro' or not(hasDepArc(pro(p), 'subj'))) { '6' }
for(i in {-3,-2,-1,0,+1,+2,+3,+4}) { '7:'+i+t(n(pro(p),i)), '8:'+i+l(n(pro(p),i)), '9:'+i+l(parent(n(pro(p),i))) }
'10:'+pathToString(path(p)), end := last(path(p)), resumptives := rDescendants(child(end))
if(l(end) != 'ROOT') {
    if(size(resumptives) > 0) {'11a' } else {'11b'+(size(pDescendants(child(end))) > 0)}
    for(s in split(l(head(end)), '_')) '12:'+s, for(arc in path(p)) { '13'+l(arc) }
    '14:'+t(head(end)), '15:'+l(head(end)), '16:'+l(parent(head(end)))
    '17:'+t(child(end)), '18:'+l(child(end)), '19:'+l(parent(child(end)))
    if(l(child(end)) = 'VB_PV' and size(suffixes(child(end)))=0) { '20' }
    for(suff in suffixes(head(end))) { for(s in split(l(suff), '_')) { '21:'+suff }} }
```

Figure 1: Pseudocode for feature production. Statements in bold font produce strings that are used to identify features. The feature set consists of all pairwise combinations of these strings.

personal pronoun and inflectional verbal affix[6] within a given sentence, these actions being *label-as-"resumptive"* and *label-as-"not-resumptive"*. The highest scored action is performed and the newly-labeled pronoun or affix is removed from further processing.

The system scores each action by computing the dot product between the feature vector derived for the pronoun/inflectional affix and the weight vector. The feature vectors consist entirely of Boolean values, each of which indicates the presence or absence of a particular feature. Each feature is identified by a unique string and these strings are generated using the pseudocode presented in Figure 1. (All pairwise combinations of the strings generated by the pseudocode are included as features.)

For space reasons, we omit a review of the training procedure for the structured perceptron and refer the interested reader to work by Goldberg and Elhadad (2010).

[6]Occasionally an imperfect verb will have both a written inflectional prefix and a written inflectional suffix. For these cases, the system only considers the prefix as there is no need to make two separate judgments.

## 6 Experiments

We trained our system on the training data using the gold standard clitic segmentation, parse, and part-of-speech information and optimized it for overall F1 (pronouns and inflectional affixes combined) on the development data. Performance peaked on training iteration 8, and we applied the resulting model to two treatments of the test data, once using the gold standard annotation and once using the Tratz (2013) Arabic NLP system to automatically pre-process the data.

### 6.1 Results and Discussion

The scores for the development and test sections, both for gold and automatic annotation, are presented in Table 4.

The system performs well when given input with gold standard clitic segmentation, POS tags, and dependency parses, achieving 91.9 F1 for resumptive pronouns on the test set and 95.4 F1 for the affixes. Performance however degrades substantially when automatic pre-processing of the source is input instead. Some of this drop can be explained by the use of gold standard markup in training—more weight was likely assigned to

| | | Pronoun | | | Inflectional Affix | | |
|---|---|---|---|---|---|---|---|
| | | **P** | **R** | **F1** | **P** | **R** | **F1** |
| Dev | Gold | 92.5 | 92.8 | 92.6 | 96.7 | 96.4 | 96.5 |
| | Auto | 88.0 | 81.0 | 84.4 | 86.1 | 77.3 | 81.5 |
| Test | Gold | 92.1 | 91.7 | 91.9 | 95.0 | 95.9 | 95.4 |
| | Auto | 83.6 | 72.8 | 77.8 | 86.6 | 76.0 | 81.0 |

Table 4: Precision, recall, and F1 results for the "is-resumptive" label on the development and test sets for gold standard clitic separation/POS tagging/parsing and automatic preprocessing.

parse and POS tag-related features than would have if automatic pre-processing of the source had been used in training.

Having examined the classification system errors on the development data, we conclude that the main source of this drop is due to poor identification and attachment of bare relatives[7] by the Tratz (2013) NLP system. While the NLP system achieves 88.5 UAS and 86.1 LAS on the development section,[8] its performance on identifying bare relatives is comparatively low, with 70.0 precision and 60.5 recall. For the test section, the NLP system performance on bare relatives is even lower at 69.6 precision and 52.7 recall. This helps to explain why our resumptive pronoun classifier performs worse on the test data than on the development data when using automatic pre-processing but not when using gold standard markup.

## 7 Related Work

The computational linguistics research most relevant to ours is the work on identifying empty categories for several languages, including English, Chinese, Korean, and Hindi. Empty categories are nodes in a parse tree that do not correspond to any written morpheme; these are used to handle several linguistic phenomena, including pro-drop. Recent research demonstrates that recovery of empty categories can lead to improved translation quality for some language pairs (Chung and Gildea, 2010; Xiang et al., 2013). For more information on the recovery of empty categories, we refer the interested reader to work by Kukkadapu and Mannem (2013), Cai et al. (2011), Yang and Xue (2010), Gabbard et al. (2006), Schmid (2006), Dienes and Dubey (2003), and Johnson (2002).

[7] Relative clauses lacking a relative pronoun. As explained in Section 2, MSA lacks relative pronouns for relative clauses modifying indefinite noun phrases.

[8] UAS and LAS stand for unlabeled and labeled attachment scores.

## 8 Conclusion

In this paper, we present the challenge of translating MSA relative clauses, which often contain resumptive pronouns, into English, which relies on (inferred) empty categories instead. We examine errors made by a popular online translation service on MSA relative clauses and present an automatic system for identifying MSA resumptive pronouns.

The online translation service occasionally generates English pronouns corresponding to MSA resumptive pronouns, producing resumptive pronouns for only 37 of 300 examples that cover a variety of frequent MSA relative clause structures.

Our MSA resumptive pronoun identification system achieves high levels of precision (92.1) and recall (91.7) on resumptive pronoun identification when using gold standard markup. Performance drops significantly when using automatic pre-processing, with precision and recall falling to 83.6 and 72.8, respectively. One of the sources of the drop appears to be the weak performance of the Tratz (2013) Arabic NLP system in identifying and attaching bare relative clauses—that is, relative clauses that lack a relative pronoun.

This work is the first attempt we are aware of to automatically identify resumptive pronouns in any language, and it presents a baseline for comparison for future research efforts.

## 9 Future Work

Going forward, we plan to experiment with applying our resumptive pronoun identifier to enhance MT performance, likely by deleting all resumptive pronouns during alignment and, again, at translation time. Another natural next step is to train the system using automatically generated parse, part-of-speech tag, and clitic segmentation information instead of gold standard annotation to see if this produces a similar drop in performance. We also plan to investigate the use of frame information of Arabic VerbNet (Mousser, 2010) as features, and we would like to focus in greater detail on the difficulties in generating resumptive pronouns when translating from English into MSA.

## References

Elsaid Badawi, Michael G. Carter, and Adrian Gully. 2004. *Modern Wrtitten Arabic: A Comprehensive Grammar*. Psychology Press.

Shu Cai, David Chiang, and Yoav Goldberg. 2011. Language-independent parsing with empty elements. In *ACL (Short Papers)*, pages 212–216.

Tagyoung Chung and Daniel Gildea. 2010. Effects of empty categories on machine translation. In *Proceedings of the 2010 Conference on Empirical Methods in Natural Language Processing*, pages 636–645.

Michael J. Collins. 2002. Discriminative Training Methods for Hidden Markov Models: Theory and experiments with Perceptron Algorithms. In *Proceedings of the 2002 Conference on Empirical Methods in Natural Language Processing*.

Péter Dienes and Amit Dubey. 2003. Antecedent recovery: Experiments with a trace tagger. In *Proceedings of the 2003 conference on Empirical methods in natural language processing*, pages 33–40.

Ryan Gabbard, Mitchell Marcus, and Seth Kulick. 2006. Fully parsing the penn treebank. In *Proceedings of the Main Conference on Human Language Technology Conference of the North American Chapter of the Association of Computational Linguistics*, pages 184–191.

Y. Goldberg and M. Elhadad. 2010. An efficient algorithm for easy-first non-directional dependency parsing. In *HLT-NAACL 2010*.

Mark Johnson. 2002. A simple pattern-matching algorithm for recovering empty nodes and their antecedents. In *Proceedings of the 40th Annual Meeting on Association for Computational Linguistics*, pages 136–143.

Puneeth Kukkadapu and Prashanth Mannem. 2013. A statistical approach to prediction of empty categories in hindi dependency treebank. In *Fourth Workshop on Statistical Parsing of Morphologically Rich Languages*, page 91.

Mohamed Maamouri and Ann Bies. 2004. Developing an Arabic Treebank: Methods, Guidelines, Procedures, and Tools. In *Proceedings of the Workshop on Computational Approaches to Arabic Script-based languages*, pages 2–9.

Mohamed Maamouri, Ann Bies, Tim Buckwalter, and Wigdan Mekki. 2004. The Penn Arabic Treebank: Building a Large-Scale Annotated Arabic Corpus. In *NEMLAR Conference on Arabic Language Resources and Tools*, pages 102–109.

Jaouad Mousser. 2010. A Large Coverage Verb Taxonomy for Arabic. In *Proceedings of the 7th International Conference on Language Resources and Evaluation*.

Karin C. Ryding. 2005. *A Reference Grammar of Modern Standard Arabic*. Cambridge University Press.

Helmut Schmid. 2006. Trace prediction and recovery with unlexicalized pcfgs and slash features. In *Proceedings of the 21st International Conference on Computational Linguistics and the 44th Annual Meeting of the Association for Computational Linguistics*, pages 177–184.

Stephen Tratz. 2013. A cross-task flexible transition model for arabic tokenization, affix detection, affix labeling, pos tagging, and dependency parsing. In *Fourth Workshop on Statistical Parsing of Morphologically Rich Languages*.

Bing Xiang, Xiaoqiang Luo, and Bowen Zhou. 2013. Enlisting the Ghost: Modeling Empty Categories for Machine Translation. In *Proceedings of the 51st Annual Meeting of the Association for Computational Linguistic*.

Yaqin Yang and Nianwen Xue. 2010. Chasing the ghost: recovering empty categories in the chinese treebank. In *Proceedings of the 23rd International Conference on Computational Linguistics: Posters*, pages 1382–1390.

# Automatic Building and Using Parallel Resources for SMT from Comparable Corpora

**Santanu Pal**[1], **Partha Pakray**[2], **Sudip Kumar Naskar**[3]
[1]Universität Des Saarlandes, Saarbrücken, Germany
[2]Computer & Information Science,
Norwegian University of Science and Technology, Trondheim, Norway
[3]Department of Computer Science & Engineering,
Jadavpur University, Kolkata, India
[1]santanu.pal@uni-saarland.de,
[2]partha.pakray@idi.ntnu.no,
[3]sudip.naskar@cse.jdvu.ac.in

## Abstract

Building parallel resources for corpus based machine translation, especially Statistical Machine Translation (SMT), from comparable corpora has recently received wide attention in the field Machine Translation research. In this paper, we propose an automatic approach for extraction of parallel fragments from comparable corpora. The comparable corpora are collected from Wikipedia documents and this approach exploits the multilingualism of Wikipedia. The automatic alignment process of parallel text fragments uses a textual entailment technique and Phrase Based SMT (PB-SMT) system. The parallel text fragments extracted thus are used as additional parallel translation examples to complement the training data for a PB-SMT system. The additional training data extracted from comparable corpora provided significant improvements in terms of translation quality over the baseline as measured by BLEU.

## 1 Introduction

Comparable corpora have recently attracted huge interest in natural language processing research. Comparable corpora are now considered as a rich resource for acquiring parallel resources such as parallel corpus or parallel text fragments,. Parallel text extracted from comparable corpora can take an important role in improving the quality of machine translation (MT) (Smith et al. 2010). Parallel text extracted from comparable corpora are typically added with the training corpus as additional training material which is expected to facilitate better performance of SMT systems specifically for low density language pairs.

In the present work, we try to extract English−Bengali parallel fragments of text from comparable corpora. We have collected document aligned corpus of English−Bengali document pairs from Wikipedia which provides a huge collection of documents in many different languages. For automatic alignment of parallel fragments we have used two-way textual entailment (TE) system and a baseline SMT system.

Textual entailment (TE), introduced by (Dagan and Glickman, 2004), is defined as a directional relationship between pairs of text expressions, denoted by the entailing *text* (T) and the entailed *hypothesis* (H). T entails H if the meaning of H can be inferred from the meaning of T. Textual Entailment has many applications in NLP tasks, such as summarization, information extraction, question answering, information retrieval, machine translation, etc. In machine translation, textual entailment can be applied to MT evaluation (Pado et al., 2009). A number of research works have been carried out on cross-lingual Textual entailment using MT (Mehdad et al.,2010; Negri et al., 2010; Neogi et al., 2012). However, to the best of our knowledge, the work presented here is the first attempt towards employing textual entailment for the purpose of extracting parallel text fragments from comparable corpora which in turn are used to improve MT system.

Munteanu and Marcu (2006) suggested that comparable corpora tend to have parallel data at sub-sentential level. Hence, instead of finding sentence level parallel resource from comparable corpora, in the present work we mainly focus on finding parallel fragments of text.

We carried out the task of automatic alignment of parallel fragments using three steps: (i) mining comparable corpora form Wikipedia, (ii) sentence level alignment using two-way TE and a baseline Bengali–English SMT system, and finally (iii) clustering the parallel sentence aligned comparable corpora using textual entailment and then aligning parallel fragments of text by textual entailment and a baseline Bengali–English SMT system.

Although, we have collected document aligned comparable corpora, the documents in the corpus do not belong to any particular domain. Even with such a corpus we have been able to improve the performance of an existing machine translation system which was built on tourism domain data. This also signifies the contribution of this work towards domain adaptation of MT systems.

The rest of the paper is organized as follows. Section 2 describes the related work. Section 3 describes the mining process of the comparable corpora. The two-way TE system architecture is described in section 4. Section 5 describes the automatic alignment technique of parallel fragment of texts. Section 6 describes the tools and resources used for this work. The experiments and evaluation results are presented in section 7. Section 8 concludes and presents avenues for future work.

## 2 Related Work

Comparable corpora have been used in many research areas in NLP, especially in machine translation. Several earlier works have studied the use of comparable corpora in machine translation. However, most of these approaches (Fung and McKeown, 1997; Fung and Yee, 1998; Rapp, 1999; Chiao and Zweigenbaum, 2002; Dejean et al., 2002; Kaji, 2005; Otero, 2007; Saralegui et al., 2008; Gupta et al., 2013) are specifically focused on extracting word translations from comparable corpora. Most of the strategies follow a standard method based on the context vector similarity measure such as finding the target words that have the most similar distributions with a given source word. In most of the cases, a starting list contains the "seed expressions" and this list is required to build the context vectors of the words in both the languages. A bilingual dictionary can be used as a starting list. The bilingual list can also be prepared form parallel corpus using bilingual correlation method (Otero, 2007). Instead of a bilingual list, multilingual thesaurus could also be used for this purpose (Dejean, 2002).

Wikipedia is a multilingual encyclopedia available in different languages and it can be used as a source of comparable corpora. Otero et al. (2010) stored the entire Wikipedia for any two languages and transformed it into a new collection: CorpusPedia. Our work shows that only a small ad-hoc corpus containing Wikipedia articles could prove to be beneficial for existing MT systems.

In the NIST shared task on Recognizing Textual Entailment Challenge (RTE), several methods have been proposed to tackle the textual entailment problem. Most of these systems use some form of lexical matching, e.g., n-gram, word similarity, etc. and even simple word overlap. A number of systems represent the texts as parse trees (e.g., syntactic or dependency trees) before the actual task. Some of the systems use semantic features (e.g., logical inference, Semantic Role Labelling) for solving the text and hypothesis entailment problem. MacCartney et al. (2006) proposed a new architecture for textual inference in which finding a good alignment is separated from evaluating entailment. Agichtein et al. (2008) presented a supervised machine learning approach to train a classifier over a variety of lexical, syntactic, and semantic metrics. Malakasiotis (2009) used string similarity measures applied to shallow abstractions of the input sentences and a Maximum Entropy classifier to learn how to combine the resulting features.

In the present work, we used the textual entailment system of Pakray et al. (2011) which performed well on various RTE tasks and datasets, as well as other NLP tasks like question answering, summarization, etc. We integrated a new module to by using reVerb [1] tool and optimized all the features produced by different modules.

The main objective of the present work is to investigate whether textual entailment can be used to establish alignments between text fragments in comparable corpora and whether the parallel text fragments extracted thus can improve MT system performance.

## 3 Mining Comparable Corpora

We collected comparable corpora from Wikipedia - online collaborative encyclopedia available in a wide variety of languages. English Wikipedia contains largest volume of data such as millions of articles; there are many language editions with at least 100,000 articles. Wikipedia links articles on the same topic in different languages using "interwiki" linking facility. Wikipedia is an enormously useful re-source for extracting parallel resources as the documents in different languages are already aligned. We first collect an English document from Wikipedia and then find the same document in Bengali if there exists any inter-language link. Extracted English–Bengali document pairs from Wikipedia are already comparable since they are written about the same entity. Although each English–Bengali document pairs are comparable and they discuss about the same topic, most of the times they are not exact translation of each other; as a result parallel fragments of text are rarely found in these document pairs. The bigger the size of the fragment may result less probable parallel version will be found in the target side. Nevertheless, there is always chance of getting parallel phrase, tokens or even sentences in comparable documents.

We designed a crawler to collect comparable corpora for English–Bengali document pairs. Based on an initial seed keyword list, the crawler first visits each English page of Wikipedia, saves the raw text (in HTML format), and then follows the cross-lingual link for each English page and collects the corresponding Bengali document. In this way, we collect English–Bengali comparable documents in the tourism domain. We retain only the textual information and all the other details are discarded. We extract English and Bengali sentences from each document. The extracted sentences from each English document are not parallel with the corresponding Bengali document. Moreover, Bengali documents are contained limited information compare to the English document. We align sentences of English–Bengali from these comparable corpora through a baseline PB-SMT system. A Bengali-English baseline PB-SMT system has been developed which was trained on English–Bengali tourism domain corpus. We translated Bengali sentences into English. The translated sentence is then examined for entailment in the English comparable document by using two-way TE system proposed in section 4. If it is more than 50% entailed with the target document then the target sentence is directly fetched form the comparable English document and the source-target sentence pair are saved in a list. In this way, we extract parallel sentences from comparable corpora. These parallel sentences except those are 100% entailed may

[1] http://reverb.cs.washington.edu/

not be completely parallel but they are comparable. So, we created a parallel fragment list which is proposed in section 5.

## 4 Two-way Textual Entailment System

A two-way automatic textual entailment (TE) recognition system that uses lexical, syntactic and semantic features has been described in this section. The system architecture has been shown in Figure 1. The TE system has used the Support Vector Machine (SVM) technique that uses thirty-one features for training purpose. In lexical module there are eighteen features and eleven features from syntactic module, one feature by using reVerb and one feature from semantic module.

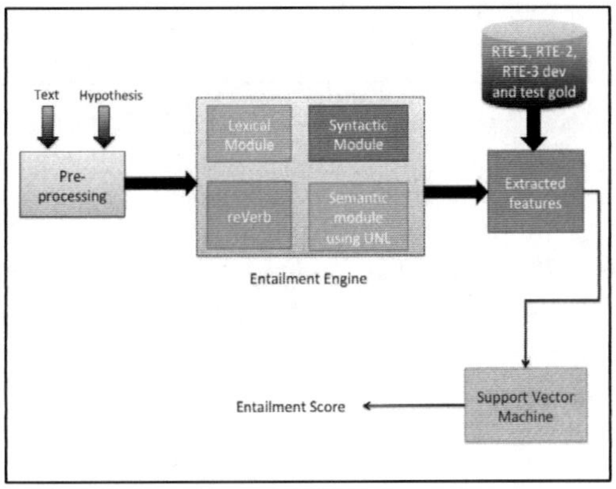


Fig.1 Two way TE architecture

### 4.1 Lexical Module

In this module six lexical comparisons and seventeen lexical distance comparisons between text and hypothesis has used.

Six lexical comparisons are WordNet (Fellbaum, 1998) based unigram match, bigram match, longest common sub-sequence, skip-gram, stemming and named entity matching. We have calculated weight from each of these six comparisons in equation (1).

$$weight = \frac{\sum number-of-common-tokens-between-text-and-hypothesis}{\sum number-of-tokens-in-hypothesis} \quad (1)$$

The API for WordNet Searching (JAWS)[2] provides Java applications with the ability to retrieve data from the WordNet 2.1 database.

For Named entity detection we have used Text Tokenization Toolkit (LT-TTT2)[3] (Grover et. al., 1999). The LT-TTT2 named entity component has been used.

For lexical distance measure, we have used features of Vector Space Measures (Euclidean distance, Block distance, Minkowsky distance, Cosine similarity, Matching Coefficient), Set-based Similarities (Dice, Jaccard, Overlap, Harmonic), Edit Distance Measures (Levenshtein distance, Smith-Waterman distance, Jaro Distance). Lexical distance measurement has used the libraries SimMetrics[4], SimPack[5] and SecondString[6]. SimMetrics is a Similarity Metric Library, e.g., from edit distance (Levenshtein, Gotoh, Jaro etc) to other metrics, (e.g Soundex, Chapman).

### 4.2 Syntactic Module

The syntactic module compares the dependency relations in both hypothesis and text. The system extracts syntactic structures from the text-hypothesis pairs using Combinatory Categorial Grammar (C&C CCG) Parser[7] and Stanford Parser[8] and compares the corresponding structures to determine if the entailment relation is established. Two different systems have been implemented one system used Stanford Parser output and another system used C&C CCG Parser. The system accepts pairs of text snippets (text and hypothesis) at the input and gives score for each comparison. Some of the important comparisons on the dependency structures of the text and the hypothesis are Subject-subject comparison, WordNet Based Subject-Verb

---

[2] http://lyle.smu.edu/~tspell/jaws/index.html
[3] http://www.ltg.ed.ac.uk/software/lt-ttt2
[4] http://sourceforge.net/projects/simmetrics/
[5]https://files.ifi.uzh.ch/ddis/oldweb/ddis/research/simpack/index.html
[6] http://sourceforge.net/projects/secondstring/
[7] http://svn.ask.it.usyd.edu.au/trac/candc/wiki
[8] http://nlp.stanford.edu/software/lex-parser.shtml

Comparison, Subject-Subject Comparison, Object-Verb Comparison, WordNet Based Object-Verb Comparison, Cross Subject-Object Comparison Number Comparison, Noun Comparison, Prepositional Phrase Comparison, Determiner Comparison and other relation Comparison.

### 4.3 reVerb Module

ReVerb [9] is a tool, which extracts binary relationships from English sentences. The extraction format is in Table 1.

| | |
|---|---|
| **Extraction Format** | arg1 rel arg2 |
| **Example** | A person is playing a guitar |
| **reVerb Extracts** | arg1= {A person} rel = {is playing} arg2 = {a guitar} |

Table **1**: Example by reVerb Tool

The system parsed the text and the hypothesis by reverb tool. Each of the relations compares between text and hypothesis and calculates a score for each pair.

### 4.4 Semantic Module

The semantic module based on the Universal Networking Language (UNL) (Uchida and Zhu, 2001). The UNL can express information or knowledge in semantic network form with hyper-nodes. The UNL is like a natural language for computers to represent and process human knowledge. There are two modules in UNL system - En-converter and De-converter module. The process of representing natural language sentences in UNL graphs is called En-converting and the process of generating natural language sentences out of UNL graphs is called De-converting. An En-Converter is a language independent parser, which provides a framework for morphological, syntactic, and semantic analysis synchronously. The En-Converter is based on a word dictionary and a set of enconversion grammar rules. It analyses sentences according to the en-conversion rules. A De-Converter is a language independent generator, which provides a framework for syntactic and morphological generation synchronously.

An example UNL relation for a sentence "*Pfizer is accused of murdering 11 children*" is shown in Table 2.

[S:00]
{org:en} *Pfizer is accused of murdering 11 children*
{/org}
{unl}
**obj**(accuse(icl>do,equ>charge,cob>abstract_thing,agt>person,obj>person).@entry
.@present,pfizer.@topic)
**qua**:01(child(icl>juvenile>thing).@pl,11)
**obj**:01(murder(icl>kill>do,agt>thing,obj>living_thing).@entry,child(icl>juvenile
>thing).@pl)
**cob**(accuse(icl>do,equ>charge,cob>abstract_thing,agt>person,obj>person).@entr
y.@present,:01)
{/unl}
[/S]

Table **2**: Example of UNL

The system converts the text and the hypothesis into UNL relations by En-Converter. Then it compares the UNL relations in both the text and the hypothesis and gives a score for each comparison.

### 4.5 Feature Extraction Module

The features are listed in Table 3:

| Name of Features | No of features |
|---|---|
| Lexical Module | 18 |
| Syntactic Module | 11 |
| reVerb Module | 1 |
| Semantic Module | 1 |

Table **3**: Features for SVM

### 4.6 Support Vector Machines (SVM)

Support Vector Machines (SVMs) [10] are supervised learning models used for classification and regression analysis. The basic SVM takes a set of input data and predicts, for

[9] http://reverb.cs.washington.edu/

[10] http://en.wikipedia.org/wiki/Support_vector_machine

each given input, which of two possible classes form the output, making it a non-probabilistic binary linear classifier.

The SVM based our Textual Entailment system has used the following data sets: RTE-1 development and RTE-1 annotated test set, RTE-2 development set and RTE-2 annotated test set, RTE-3 development set and RTE-3 annotated test set to deal with the two-way classification task. The system has used the LIBSVM -- A Library for Support Vector Machines[11] for the classifier to learn from this data set.

## 5 Alignment of Parallel fragments using proposed TE system

We have extracted parallel fragment from the parallel sentence aligned comparable resource list as well as the training data. Initially, we make cluster on the English side of this list with the help of two-way TE method. More than 50% entailed sentences have been considered to take a part of the same cluster. The TE system divides the complete set of comparable resources list into some smaller sets of cluster. Each cluster contains at least two English sentences. Each English cluster is corresponding to the set comparable Bengali sentences. So in this way we have developed a number of English Bengali parallel clusters. We intersect between the both English and Bengali sentences which are belonging to the same clusters.

We try to align the English and Bengali fragments extracted from a parallel sentence aligned comparable resource list. If both sides contain only one fragment then the alignment is trivial, and we add such fragment pairs to seed another parallel fragment corpus that contains examples having only one token in both side. Otherwise, we establish alignments between the English and Bengali fragments using translation. If both the English and Bengali side contains $n$ number of fragments, and the alignments of $n$-1 fragments can be established through translation or by means of already existing alignments, then the $n^{th}$ alignment is trivial.

These parallel fragments of text, extracted from the comparable corpora are added with the tourism domain training corpus to enhance the performance of the baseline PB-SMT system.

## 6 Tools and Resources

A sentence-aligned English–Bengali parallel corpus contains 23,492 parallel sentences from the travel and tourism domain has been used in the present work. The corpus has been collected from the consortium-mode project "Development of English to Indian Languages Machine Translation (EILMT) System[12]". The Stanford Parser[13] and CRF chunker[14] (Xuan-Hieu Phan, 2006) have been used for parsing and chunking in the source side of the parallel corpus, respectively.

The experiments were carried out using the standard log-linear PB-SMT model as our baseline system: GIZA++ implementation of IBM word alignment model 4, phrase-extraction heuristics described in (Koehn et al., 2003), minimum-error-rate training (Och, 2003) on a held-out development set, target language model trained using SRILM toolkit (Stolcke, 2002) with Kneser-Ney smoothing (Kneser and Ney, 1995) and the Moses decoder (Koehn et al., 2007) have been used in the present study.

## 7 Experiments and Results

We randomly identified 500 sentences each for the development set and the test set from the initial parallel corpus. The rest is considered as the training corpus. The training corpus was filtered with the maximum allowable sentence length of 100 words and sentence length ratio of 1:2 (either way). Finally the training corpus

[11] http://www.csie.ntu.edu.tw/~cjlin/libsvm/

[12] The EILMT project is funded by the Department of Electronics and Information Technology (DEITY), Ministry of Communications and Information Technology (MCIT), Government of India.

[13] http://nlp.stanford.edu/software/lex-parser.shtml

[14] http://crfchunker.sourceforge.net/

contained 22,492 sentences. In addition to the target side of the parallel corpus, we used a monolingual Bengali corpus containing 488,026 words from the tourism domain for building the target language model. Experiments were carried out with different n-gram settings for the language model and the maximum phrase length and it was found that a 4-gram language model and a maximum phrase length of 7 produce the optimum baseline result on both the development and the test set. We carried out the rest of the experiments using these settings.

The collected comparable corpus consisted of 5582 English–Bengali document pairs. It is evident from Table 4 that English documents are more informative than the Bengali documents as the number of sentences in English documents is much higher than those in the Bengali documents. When the Bengali fragments of texts were passed to the Bengali–English translation module some of them could not be translated into English and also, some of them could be translated only partially. Therefore, some of the tokens were translated while some were not. Some of those partially translated text fragments were aligned through textual entailment; however, most of them were discarded. As can be seen from Table 4, 9,117 sentences were entailed in the English side, of which the system was able to establish cross-lingual entailment for 2,361 English–Bengali sentence pairs.

| | **No. of English sentence** | **No. of Bengali sentence** |
|---|---|---|
| **Extraction from Comparable corpora** | 579037 | 169978 |
| **more than 50% Entailed English Sentences** | 9117 | - |
| **more than 50% Entailed (sentence aligned comparable)** | 2361 | 2361 |
| **parallel fragment of texts from sentence aligned comparable list** | 3937 | 3937 |

Table 4: Statistics of the sentence aligned comparable list and the aligned parallel text fragments.

Finally, the textual entailment based alignment procedure was able to align 3937 parallel fragments as reported in Table 4. Manual inspection of the parallel list revealed that most of the aligned texts were of good quality.

We carried out evaluation of the MT quality using four automatic MT evaluation metrics: BLEU (Papineni et al., 2002), METEOR (Banerjee and Lavie, 2005), NIST (Doddington, 2002) and TER (Snover et al., 2006). Table 5 shows the performance of the PB-SMT systems built on the initial training corpus and the larger training corpus containing parallel text fragments extracted from the comparable corpora. Treating the parallel text fragments extracted from the comparable corpora as additional training material results in significant improvement in terms of BLEU (1.73 points, 15.84% relative) over the baseline system. Similar improvements are also obtained for the other metrics. The low evaluation scores could be attributed to the fact that Bengali is a morphologically rich language and has a relatively free phrase order; besides there were only one set of reference translations for the testset.

| **Experiments** | **BLEU** | **NIST** | **METEOR** | **TER** |
|---|---|---|---|---|
| Baseline | 10.92 | 4.16 | 0.3073 | 75.34 |
| Baseline + parallel fragments of texts as additional training material | 12.65 | 4.32 | 0.3144 | 73.00 |

Table 5: Evaluation results

## 8 Conclusion and Future Work

In this paper, we have successfully extracted English–Bengali parallel fragments of text from comparable corpora using textual entailment techniques. The parallel text fragments extracted thus were able to bring significant improvements in the performance of an existing machine translation system. For low density language pairs, this approach can help to improve the state-of-art machine translation quality. A manual inspection on a subset of the output revealed that the additional training material extracted from comparable corpora effectively resulted in better lexical choice and less OOV words than the baseline output. As the collected parallel text does not belong to any particular domain, this work also signifies that out of domain data is also useful to enhance the performance of a domain specific MT system. This aspect of the work would be useful for domain adaptation in MT. As future work, we would like to carry out experiments on larger datasets.

### Acknowledgments

The research leading to these results has received funding from the EU project EXPERT –the People Programme (Marie Curie Actions) of the European Union's Seventh Framework Programme FP7/2007-2013<tel:2007-2013>/ under REA grant agreement no. [317471]. We acknowledge the support from Department of Computer and Information Science, Norwegian University of Science and Technology and also support from ABCDE fellowship programme 2012-1013.

## References

Banerjee, Satanjeev and Alon Lavie. 2005. METEOR: An Automatic Metric for MT Evaluation with Improved Correlation with Human Judgments. Proceedings of the ACL Workshop on Intrinsic and Extrinsic Evaluation Measures for Machine Translation and/or Summarization, Ann Arbor, Michigan, pages 65–72.

Chiao, Yun-Chuang and Pierre Zweigenbaum. 2002. Looking for candidate translational equivalents in specialized, comparable corpora. In Proceedings of the 19th international conference on Computational linguistics, Volume 2, Association for Computational Linguistics, pages 1-5.

Dagan, Ido and Oren Glickman. 2004. Probabilistic textual entailment: generic applied modeling of language variability, In PASCAL Workshop on Learning Methods for Text Understanding and Mining, Grenoble, France.

De Marneffe, Marie-Catherine, Bill MacCartney, Trond Grenager, Daniel Cer, Anna Rafferty, and Christopher D. Manning. 2006. Learning to distinguish valid textual entailments. In B. Magnini and I. Dagan (eds.), Proceedings of the Second PASCAL Recognizing Textual Entailment Challenge. Venice: Springer, pages 74–79.

Déjean, Hervé, Éric Gaussier, and Fatia Sadat. 2002. Bilingual terminology extraction: an approach based on a multilingual thesaurus applicable to comparable corpora. In Proceedings of the 19th International Conference on Computational Linguistics COLING, Pages 218-224.

Doddington, George. 2002. Automatic evaluation of machine translation quality using n-gram co-occurrence statistics. In Proceedings of the second international conference on Human Language Technology Research . Morgan Kaufmann Publishers Inc, pages. 138-145.

Fung, Pascale and Kathleen McKeown. 1997. Finding terminology translations from non-parallel corpora. In Proceedings of the 5th Annual Workshop on Very Large Corpora, pages 192-202.

Fung, Pascale and Lo Yuen Yee. 1998. An IR approach for translating new words from nonparallel, comparable texts. In Proceedings of the 17th international conference on Computational linguistics-Volume 1, Association for Computational Linguistics, pages 414-420.

Gupta, Rajdeep, Santanu Pal, and Sivaji Bandyopadhyay. 2013. Improving MT System Using Extracted Parallel Fragments of Text from Comparable Corpora. In proceedings of 6th workshop of Building and Using Comparable Corpora (BUCC), ACL, Sofia, Bulgaria, Pages 69-76.

Kneser, Reinhard and Hermann Ney. 1995. Improved backing-off for n-gram language modeling. In Proceedings of the IEEE International Conference on Acoustics, Speech and Signal Processing, volume I. pages 181-184.

Koehn, Philipp, Hieu Hoang, Alexandra Birch, Chris Callison-Burch, Marcello Federico,Nicola Bertoldi, Brooke Cowan, Wade Shen, Christine Moran, Richard Zens, Chris Dyer, Ond rej Bojar, Alexandra Constantin, and Evan Herbst. Moses: open source toolkit for statistical machine translation. In Proceedings of the 45th Annual Meeting of the ACL on Interactive Poster and Demonstration Sessions. Association for Computational Linguistics, pages 177-180.

Koehn, Philipp, Franz Josef Och, and Daniel Marcu. 2003. Statistical phrase-based translation. In

Proceedings of the 2003 Conference of the North American Chapter of the Association for Computational Linguistics on Human Language Technology-Volume 1, Association for Computational Linguistics, pages 48-54.

Mehdad, Yashar, Matteo Negri, and Marcello Federico. 2010. Towards Cross-Lingual Textual entailment. In Proceedings of the 11th Annual Conference of the North American Chapter of the Association for Computational Linguistics, NAACL-HLT 2010. LA, USA.

Munteanu, Dragos Stefan and Daniel Marcu. 2006. Extracting parallel sub-sentential fragments from non-parallel corpora. In Proceedings of the 21st International Conference on Computational Linguistics and the 44th annual meeting of the Association for Computational Linguistics, Association for Computational Linguistics, pages 81-88.

Negri, Matteo, and Yashar Mehdad. 2010. Creating a Bilingual Entailment Corpus through Translations with Mechanical Turk: $100 for a 10-day Rush. In Proceedings of the NAACL-HLT 2010, Creating Speech and Text Language Data With Amazon's Mechanical Turk Workshop. LA, USA.

Neogi, Snehasis, Partha Pakray, Sivaji Bandyopadhyay, and Alexander Gelbukh. 2012. JU_CSE_NLP: Language Independent Cross-lingual Textual Entailment System. (*SEM) First Joint Conference on Lexical and Computational Semantics, Collocated with NAACL-HLT 2012, Montreal, Canada.

Och, F. Josef. 2003. Minimum error rate training in statistical machine translation. In Proceedings of the 41st Annual Meeting on Association for Computational Linguistics-Volume 1, Association for Computational Linguistics, pages 160-167.

Och, F. Josef and Herman Ney. 2000. Giza++: Training of statistical translation models.

Otero, P. Gamallo. 2007. Learning bilingual lexicons from comparable english and spanish corpora. Proceedings of MT Summit xI, pages 191-198.

Otero, P. Gamallo and Isaac González López. 2010. Wikipedia as multilingual source of comparable corpora. In Proceedings of the 3rd Workshop on Building and Using Comparable Corpora, LREC, pages 21-25.

Papineni, Kishore, Salim Roukos, Todd Ward, and Wei-Jing Zhu. 2002. BLEU: a method for automatic evaluation of machine translation. In Proceedings of the 40th annual meeting on association for computational linguistics, Association for Computational Linguistics, pages 311-318.

Prodromos Malakasiotis. 2009. "AUEB at TAC 2009", In TAC 2009 Workshop, National Institute of Standards and Technology Gaithersburg, Maryland USA.

Rapp, Reinhard. 1999. Automatic identification of word translations from unrelated English and German corpora. In Proceedings of the 37th annual meeting of the Association for Computational Linguistics on Computational Linguistics, Association for Computational Linguistics, pages 519-526.

Saralegui, X., San Vicente, I., and Gurrutxaga, A. 2008. Automatic generation of bilingual lexicons from comparable corpora in a popular science domain. In LREC 2008 workshop on building and using comparable corpora.

Pado, Sebastian, Michel Galley, Dan Jurafsky, and Christopher D. Manning. 2009. Textual entailment features for machine translation evaluation. In Proceedings of the EACL Workshop on Statistical Machine Translation, Athens, Greece, pages 37–41.

Smith, R. Jason, Chris Quirk, and Kristina Toutanova. 2010. Extracting parallel sentences from comparable corpora using document level alignment. In Human Language Technologies: The 2010 Annual Conference of the North American Chapter of the Association for Computational Linguistics, Association for Computational Linguistics, pages 403-411.

Snover, Matthew, Bonnie Dorr, Richard Schwartz, Linnea Micciulla, and John Makhoul. 2006. A study of translation edit rate with targeted human annotation. Proceedings of Association for Machine Translation in the Americas, Cambridge, Massachusetts, USA, pages 223–231.

Pakray, Partha, Snehasis Neogi, Pinaki Bhaskar, Soujanya Poria, Sivaji Bandyopadhyay, and Alexander Gelbukh. 2011. A Textual Entailment System using Anaphora Resolution. System Report, Text Analysis Conference Recognizing Textual Entailment Track (TAC RTE) Notebook, November 14-15, 2011, National Institute of

Standards and Technology, Gaithersburg, Maryland USA

Stolcke, Andreas. 2002. SRILM-an extensible language modeling toolkit. In Proceedings of the international conference on spoken language processing, Volume 2, pages 901-904.

Wang, Rui and Günter Neumann. 2007. Recognizing Textual Entailment Using Sentence Similarity based on Dependency Tree Skeletons. In Proceedings of the third PASCAL Recognising Textual Entailment Challenge.

Xuan-Hieu Phan. 2006. CRFChunker: CRF English Phrase Chunker , http://crfchunker.sourceforge.net/.

# Improving the precision of automatically constructed human-oriented translation dictionaries

**Alexandra Antonova**
Yandex
16, Leo Tolstoy St., Moscow, Russia
antonova@yandex-team.ru

**Alexey Misyurev**
Yandex
16, Leo Tolstoy St., Moscow, Russia
misyurev@yandex-team.ru

## Abstract

In this paper we address the problem of automatic acquisition of a human-oriented translation dictionary from a large-scale parallel corpus. The initial translation equivalents can be extracted with the help of the techniques and tools developed for the phrase-table construction in statistical machine translation. The acquired translation equivalents usually provide good lexicon coverage, but they also contain a large amount of noise. We propose a supervised learning algorithm for the detection of noisy translations, which takes into account the context and syntax features, averaged over the sentences in which a given phrase pair occurred. Across nine European language pairs the number of serious translation errors is reduced by 43.2%, compared to a baseline which uses only phrase-level statistics.

## 1 Introduction

The automatic acquisition of translation equivalents from parallel texts has been extensively studied since the 1990s. At the beginning, the acquired bilingual lexicons had much poorer quality as compared to the human-built translation dictionaries. The limited size of available parallel corpora often resulted in small coverage and the imperfections of alignment methods introduced a considerable amount of noisy translations. However, the automatimacally acquired lexicons served as internal resources for statistical machine translation (SMT) (Brown et al., 1993), information retrieval (IR) (McEvan et al., 2002; Velupillai, 2008), or computer-assisted lexicography (Atkins, 1994; Hartmann, 1994).

The current progress in search of web-based parallel documents (Resnik, 2003; Smith, 2013) makes it possible to automatically construct large-scale bilingual lexicons. These lexicons can already compare in coverage to the traditional translation dictionaries. Hence a new interesting possibility arises - to produce automatically acquired human-oriented translation dictionaries, that have a practical application. A machine translation system can output an automatically generated dictionary entry in response to the short queries. The percentage of short queries can be quite large, and the system benefits from showing several possible translations instead of a single result of machine translation (Figure 1).

Figure 1: Examples of dictionary entries in two online statistical machine translation systems.

The initial translation equivalents for a bilingual lexicon can be extracted with the help of the techniques and tools developed for the phrase-table construction in SMT. The widely used word alignment and phrase extraction algorithms are described in Brown et.al (1993) and Och (2004). Though an SMT phrase-table actually consists of translation equivalents, it may differ substantially from a traditional dictionary (Table 1).

| Human-oriented dictionary | SMT phrase-table |
|---|---|
| Lemmatized entries are preferred. | Words and phrases in all forms are acceptable. |
| Only linguistically motivated phrases are acceptable. | Any multiword phrase is acceptable. |
| Precision is important. Any noise is undesirable. | Having lots of low-probability noise is acceptable, since it is generally overridden by better translations. |

Table 1: Differences between a human-oriented dictionary and an SMT phrase-table.

While the problems of lemmatization and selection of linguistically motivated phrases can be addressed by applying appropriate morphological and syntactic tools, the problem of noise reduction is essential for the dictionary quality. The current progress in the automatic acquisition of similar Web documents in different languages (Resnik, 2003; Smith, 2013) allows to collect large-scale corpora. But the automatically found documents can be non-parallel, or contain spam, machine translation, language recognition mistakes, badly parsed HTML-markup. The noisy parallel sentences can be the source of lots of noisy translations — unrelated, misspelled, or belonging to a different language. For example, non-parallel sentences

> The apartment is at a height of 36 floors! (English)
>
> La plage est à 1 minute en voiture. (French: The beach is 1 minute by car.)

may produce a wrong translation "apartment - plage". Or, automatically translated sentences

> The figures in the foreground and background play off each other well. (English)
>
> Les chiffres du premier plan et jouer hors de l'autre bien. (French: The digits of the foreground and play out of the other well.)

may produce a wrong phrase translation "figures in the foreground - chiffres du premier plan".

An intuitive approach would be to apply noise filtering to the corpus, not to the lexicon. One could discard those sentences that deviate too much from the expected behavior. For example, sentences that have many unknown words and few symmetrically aligned words are unlikely to be really parallel. However, natural language demonstrates a great variability. A single sentence pair can deviate strongly from the expected behavior, and still contain some good translations. On the other hand, many noisy translations can still penetrate the lexicon, and further noise detection is necessary.

In a bilingual lexicon we want not just to lower the probabilities of noisy translations, but to remove them completely. This can be regarded as a binary classification task — the phrase pairs are to be classified into good and noisy ones.

Different types of information can be combined in a feature vector. We take advantage of the phrase-level features, such as co-occurrence counts or translation probabilities, and also propose a number of sentence-level context features. To calculate the sentence-level features for a given phrase-pair, we average the characteristics of all the sentences where it occurs.

We test the proposed algorithm experimentally, by constructing the bilingual lexicons for nine language pairs. The manually annotated samples of phrase pairs serve as the data for training supervised classifiers. The experiment shows that the use of the sentence-level features increases the classification accuracy, compared to a baseline which uses only phrase frequencies and translation probabilities. We compare the accuracy of different classifiers and evaluate the importance of different features.

The rest of the paper is organized as follows. In Section 2 we outline the related work. Section 3 describes our approach to the noise reduction in a bilingual lexicon and discusses the proposed features. We describe our experiments on training classifiers in Section 4. Section 5 concludes the paper.

## 2 Previous work

The methods of extracting a bilingual lexicon from parallel texts as a part of the alignment process are discussed in Brown (1993), Melamed (1996), Tufiş and Barbu (2001). Melamed (1996) proposes a method of noise reduction that allows to re-estimate and filter out indirect word associations. However, he works with a carefully prepared Hansards parallel corpus and the noise comes only from the imperfections of statistical modeling.

Sahlgren (2004) proposes a co-occurrence-based approach, representing words as high-dimensional random index vectors. The vectors of translation equivalents are expected to have high correlation. Yet, he notes that low-frequency words do not produce reliable statistics for this method.

The methods of bilingual lexicon extraction from comparable texts (Rapp, 1995; Fung, 1998; Otero, 2007) also deal with the problem of noise reduction. However, the precision/recall ratio of a lexicon extracted from comparable corpus is generally lower. For the purpose of building a human-oriented dictionary, the parallel texts may provide the larger coverage and better quality of the translation equivalents.

The noise reduction task is addressed by some of the SMT phrase-table pruning techniques. The most straightforward approach is thresholding on the translation probability (Koehn et al., 2003). Moore (2004) proposes the log-likelihood ratio and Fisher's exact test to re-estimate word association strength. Johnson et al. (2007) applies Fisher's exact test to dramatically reduce the number of phrase pairs in the phrase-table. They get rid of phrases that appear as alignment artifacts or are unlikely to occur again. The implementation of their algorithm requires a special index of all parallel corpus in order to enable a quick look-up for a given phrase pair. Eck et al. (2007) assesses the phrase pairs based on the actual usage statistics when translating a large amount of text. Entropy-based criteria are proposed in Ling et al. (2012), Zens et al. (2012).

Automatically acquired bilingual lexicons are capable to reflect many word meanings and translation patterns, which are often not obvious even to the professional lexicographers (Sharoff, 2004). Their content can also be updated regularly to incorporate more parallel texts and capture the translations of new words and expressions. Thus, the methods allowing to improve the quality of automatic bilingual lexicons are of practical importance.

## 3 Noise detection features

We treat the noise recognition task as a binary classification problem. A set of nonlexical context features is designed to be sensitive to different types of noise in the parallel corpus. We expect that the combination of these features with the phrase-level features based on co-occurrence statistics can improve the accuracy of the classification and the overall quality of a bilingual lexicon.

### 3.1 Context feature extraction algorithm

The procedure of getting the context features is outlined in Algorithm 1. Unlike Johnson et al. (2007) we do not rely on any pre-constructed index of the parallel sentences, because it requires a lot of RAM on large corpora. Instead we re-run the phrase extraction algorithm of the Moses toolkit (Koehn et al., 2007) and update the context features at the moment when a phrase pair $t$ is found.

**Algorithm 1** Calculate context features for all lexicon entries

**Require:** Parallel corpus — $C$; {word-aligned sentences}
**Require:** Bilingual lexicon — $D$; {this is a phrase-table, derived from $C$ and modified as descibed in 4.1}
**Ensure:** $V = \{\bar{v}(d) : d \in D\}$; {resulting features}
  **for all** $d \in D$ **do**
    $\bar{v}(d) \leftarrow 0$;
    $n(d) \leftarrow 0$;
  **for all** $s \in C$ **do**
    $T \leftarrow PhraseExtraction(s)$;{Moses function}
    **for all** $t \in T$ **do**
      **if** $t \in D$ **then**
        $\bar{v}(t) \leftarrow \bar{v}(t) + SentFeats(s)$; {Alg. 2}
        $n(t) \leftarrow n(t) + 1$;
  **for all** $d \in D$ **do**
    $\bar{v}(d) \leftarrow \bar{v}(d)/(1 + n(d))$; {average, +1 smoothing}
  **return** $V$

### 3.2 Sentence-level features

The phrase extraction algorithms do not preserve the information about the sentences in which a given phrase pair occurred, assuming that all the sentences are equally good. As a result, the phrase-level statistics is insufficient in case of a noisy corpus.

The sentence-level features are designed to partly restore the information which is lost during the phrase extraction process. We try to estimate the general characteristics of the whole set of parallel sentences where a given phrase pair occurred. The proposed sentence-level features rely on the different sources of information, which are discussed in 3.2.1, 3.2.2 and 3.2.3. Table 2 provides illustrating examples of noisy phrase pairs and sample sentences.

### 3.2.1 Word-alignment annotation

We use the intersection of direct and reverse Giza++ (Och and Ney, 2004) alignments as a heuristic rule to find words reliably aligned to each other. The alignment information gives rise to several sentence-level features:

- $UnsafeAlign$ - percentage of words that are not symmetrically aligned to each other.
- $UnsafeJump$ - average distance between the translations of subsequent input words.
- $UnsafeDigAlign$ percentage of unequal digits among the symmetrically aligned words.

The $UnsafeAlign$ and $UnsafeJump$ values can vary in different sentences. However, their being too large on the whole set of sentences where a given phrase pair occurred possibly indicates some systematic noise.

The translations of digits are not included to the dictionary by themselves. But if a pair of digits is wrongly aligned, then its nearest context may also be aligned wrongly.

### 3.2.2 One-side morphological and syntactic annotation

The target side of our parallel sentences has been processed by a rule-based parser. The syntax gives rise to:

- $UnsafeStruct$ - percentage of words having no dependence on any other word in the parse tree.

The morphological annotation participates in:

- $OOV$ - percentage of out-of-vocabulary words in the sentence.

The low parse tree connectivity may indicate that the sentence is ungrammatical or produced by a poor-quality machine translation system. Sentences containing many out-of-vocabulary words probably do not belong to the given language. We compute out-of-vocabulary words according to an external vocabulary, which is embedded in tagging and parsing tools. However, instead one can use a collection of unigrams filtered by some frequency threshold..

| |
|---|
| **gratuit — internet access**, $S_{lem} = 215$<br>Sample sentence:<br>*Petit déjeuner continental de luxe gratuit*<br>*Business center with free wireless Internet access*<br>$UnsafeAlign = 0.387$ |
| **à — you**, $S_{lem} = 586$<br>*La plainte à transmettre*<br>*You should submit your complaint*<br>$UnsafeJump = 1.75$ |
| **juin — May**, $S_{lem} = 35$<br>*Membre depuis: 17 juin 2011*<br>*Member since: 01 May 2012*<br>$UnsafeAlignDig = 0.08$ |
| **le — Fr**, $S_{lem} = 24$<br>*Edvaldo et le père Antenore*<br>*Edvaldo and Fr Antenore*<br>$OOV = 0.117$ |
| **Paris — England**, $S_{lem} = 54$<br>*TERTIALIS (Paris, Paris)*<br>*(England)*<br>$Punct = 0.117$ |

Table 2: Examples of noisy French-English translations to which different sentence-level features may be sensitive. $S_{lem}$ — is the number of sentences where a lemmatized phrase pair co-occurred. Sample sentences are provided.

### 3.2.3 Surface text

The surface word tokens can be used for:

- $Punct$ - percentage of non-word/punctuation tokens in the sentence.
- $Uniqueness$ - the percentage of unique unigrams in both source and target language sentences.

Sentences with lots of punctuation can be unnatural or contain enumeration. Large enumeration lists are often not exactly parallel and can be aligned incorrectly, because punctuation tokens, like many commas, are easily mapped to each other. The low $Uniqueness$ possibly indicates that the sentences containing a given phrase pair are similar to each other. This can lead to overestimated translation probabilities.

---

**Algorithm 2** Get features of one sentence pair ($SentFeats$)

**Require:** $sent_{src} = (w_1, ..., w_m)$;
**Require:** $sent_{dst} = (w_1, ..., w_n)$;
**Require:** Alignment matrix — $M_{m,n} : x \in \{0, 1\}$; {intersection of two Giza++ alignments}
**Require:** $oov = (x_1, ..., x_n), x \in \{0, 1\}$; $\{x_i = 1 \iff sent_{dst}[i]$ is out-of-vocabulary$\}$
**Require:** $pnt = (x_1, ..., x_n), x \in \{0, 1\}$; $\{x_i = 1 \iff sent_{dst}[i]$ is punctuation$\}$
**Require:** $nohead = (x_1, ..., x_n), x \in \{0, 1\}$; $\{x_i = 1 \iff sent_{dst}[i]$ is not dependent on any other word in the parse$\}$
**Ensure:** $\bar{v} = (v_1, ..., v_7)$; {features}
  $\bar{v} \leftarrow 0$;
  $v_2 \leftarrow \frac{1}{n} \sum\limits_{x \in nohead} x$; $\{UnsafeStruct\}$
  Let $A$ be the set of pairs of indices of symmetrically aligned words, ordered by the source indices:
  $A \leftarrow \{(i, j) \mid M(i, j) = 1\}$;
  $v_3 \leftarrow 1 - \frac{|A|}{m+n}$; $\{UnsafeAlign\}$
  **for all** $(i, j) \in A$ **do**
    **if** words with indices $i$, $j$ are unequal digits **then**
      $v_4 \leftarrow v_4 + 1$;
  $v_4 \leftarrow \frac{v_4}{|A|}$; $\{UnsafeAlignDig\}$
  $v_5 \leftarrow \frac{1}{|A|} \sum_{(i,j) \in A} j_i - j_{i-1}$; $\{UnsafeJump\}$
  $v_6 \leftarrow \frac{1}{n} \sum\limits_{x \in oov} x$; $\{OOV\}$
  $v_7 \leftarrow \frac{1}{n} \sum\limits_{x \in pnt} x$; $\{Punct\}$
  **return** $\bar{v}$

---

### 3.3 Phrase-level statistics

Multiple phrase-level features can be derived from the occurrence and co-occurrence counts, that are calculated during the phrase extraction procedure as described in Koehn et. al (2003).

- $C(f), C(e), C(e, f)$ — surface phrase occurrence counts.
- $C_{lem}(f)$, $C_{lem}(e)$, $C_{lem}(e, f)$ — same for lemmatized phrases.
- $S(e, f)$, $S_{lem}(e, f)$ — the number of sentences, in which the surface (or lemmatized) phrases co-occurred.
- $P(e|f)$, $P(f|e)$ — translation probabilities of surface phrases.
- $P_{lem}(e|f)$, $P_{lem}(f|e)$ — translation probabilities of lemmatized phrases.

Some of these features are highly correlated, and it is hard to tell in advance which subset leads to better performance.

## 4 Experiment

We conducted experiments on nine language pairs: German-English, German-Russian, French-English, French-Russian, Italian-English, Italian-Russian, Spanish-English, Spanish-Russian and English-Russian. The parallel corpora consisted of the sentence-aligned documents automatically collected from multilingual web-sites.

We implemented the procedure of bilingual lexicon construction and the algorithm calculating the sentence-level features (Section 3).

The annotated phrase pair samples, one for each language pair, provided positive and negative examples for training a supervised classifier. We compared the accuracy of several classifiers trained on different feature sets. The importance of different features was evaluated .

### 4.1 Bilingual lexicon creation

We used Giza++ for word alignment and Moses toolkit for phrase extraction procedure. The following automatic annotation had been provided. The source side of the parallel corpora had been processed by a part-of-speech tagger, and each word had been assigned a lemma based on its tag. The target side of the parallel corpora, which was always either English or Russian, was processed by a rule-based dependency parser, which also supplied morphological annotations and lemmas. In the case of English-Russian corpus, the source side had also been processed by the parser.

The extracted English phrases were restricted to at most 3 words, provided that they were connected in the dependency tree. The same restrictions were imposed on the Russian phrases. The extracted phrases for all other languages were restricted to single words to avoid the ungrammatical multiword expressions.

Each extracted phrase pair was assigned a lemmatized key consisting of lemmas of all words in it. The co-occurrence counts were summed over all phrase pairs sharing the same key, giving the aggregate count $C_{lem}(e, f)$. Then a single pair was chosen to serve as a best substitute for a lemmatized lexicon entry. The choice was made heuristically, based on the morphological attributes and co-occurrence counts.

As a preliminary lexicon cleanup we removed the phrase pairs which contained punctuation symbols or digits on either side. We also removed the pairs that co-occurred only once in the corpus. An example of differences between the size of original phrase table and the size of bilingual lexicon after lemmatization and preliminary cleanup is represented in Table 3.

| | Millions of phrase pairs | |
|---|---|---|
| | fr-en | fr-ru |
| Initial 1-3 phrase-table | 16.4 | 30.8 |
| After lemmatization | 7.9 | 6.4 |
| After preliminary cleanup | 1.6 | 0.8 |

Table 3: The number of phrase pairs on different stages of French-English and French-Russian dictionary creation. Phrase pairs in the initial phrase table are restricted to at most 1 source word and at most 3 target words.

### 4.2 Experimental data

For the experiment we selected random[1] translation equivalents from the nine translation lexicons, to which no further noise reduction had been applied. The resulting translation equivalents were assessed by human experts. The annotation task was to determine how well a phrase pair fits for a human-oriented translation dictionary. The annotators classified each translation according to the following gradation:

Class 0 — difficult to assess.

Class 1 — totally wrong or noisy (e.g. misspelled);

Class 2 — incorrect or incomplete translation;

Class 3 — not a mistake, but unnecessary translation;

Class 4 — good, but not vital;

Class 5 — vital translation (must be present in human-built dictionary);

[1]Random was used proportionally to the square root of joint frequency, in order to balance rare and frequent phrase pairs in the sample.

The pairs annotated as 0 usually represented the translations of unfamiliar words, abbreviations and the like. Such phrases were excluded from training and testing. We didn't use "acceptable, but unnecessary" translation pairs either, because they do not influence the quality of the lexicon. We treated as negative the phrase pairs that were annotated as 1 or 2. Analogously, the positive examples had to belong to 4 or 5 class. The annotation statistics is given in Table 4.

| Language | Size | %Negative | %Positive |
|---|---|---|---|
| it-ru | 2340 | 56.6 | 28.7 |
| it-en | 2366 | 59.9 | 21.4 |
| es-ru | 2388 | 55.5 | 27.2 |
| es-en | 2384 | 69.0 | 24.0 |
| de-ru | 2397 | 50.3 | 37.6 |
| de-en | 2438 | 72.1 | 24.5 |
| fr-ru | 2461 | 44.5 | 31.2 |
| fr-en | 2325 | 57.0 | 24.4 |
| en-ru | 2346 | 27.8 | 33.2 |

Table 4: Statistics of the annotated data: the number of annotated phrase pairs, the percentage of negative and positive examples.

### 4.3 Training setting

The experiments were run with two different feature sets:

- Baseline — features based on co-occurrence counts.
- Full — baseline and sentence-level features.

We had to choose a subset of co-occurrence-based features experimentally (see, Section 3.3). The best subset for our data consisted of three features: $log(S_{lem})$, $log(P(e|f))$, $log(P(f|e))$. In the full feature set we combined the baseline features and the sentence-level features calculated as described in Algorithm 2.

We considered three metrics related to the improvement of the lexicon quality:

- Err — the percentage of prediction errors;
- Err-1 — the percentage of class 1 examples which were classified as positive.
- F1 — the harmonic mean of precision and recall w.r.t. the positive and negative examples;

We used the standard packages of the R programming language, to train and tune different classifiers: random forest (RF), support vector machines (SVM), logistic regression (GLM), Naive Bayes classifier, neural networks, k-Nearest Neighbors and some of the combinations of these methods with SVD. To assess the predictive accuracy we used repeated random sub-sampling validation. In each of 40 iterations, a 10% test set was randomly chosen from the dataset, the model was trained on the rest of the data, and then tested. The resulting accuracy was averaged over the iterations.

| Classifier | Full feature set | | Base feature set | |
|---|---|---|---|---|
| | %Err | %Err-1 | %Err | %Err-1 |
| RF | 19.80 | 8.31 | 24.00 | 14.62 |
| SVM | 19.63 | 9.36 | 23.49 | 12.91 |
| GLM | 22.74 | 6.35 | 25.23 | 7.30 |

Table 5: Percentage of prediction errors of different classifiers, averaged over the nine language pairs.

The results of RF, SVM and GLM are reported in Table 5. Though the composition of different classifiers could perform slightly better, it would require an individual tuning for each language pair. For clearness, we use a single classifier (RF) for the rest of the experiments.

The experiment showed that training on the full feature set reduced the total amount of prediction errors by 17.5%, compared to the baseline setting. The number of false positives among the class 1 examples reduced by 43%. It is also important that better results were obtained on each of the nine language pairs, not only on average. In Table 6 the baseline results are shown in brackets and one can see that F1 diminishes in the baseline setting, while the percentage of errors goes up. The classification accuracy depends on the size of the training set (Table 7).

| Lang | %Err | %Err-1 | F1 |
|---|---|---|---|
| de-en | 18.0 (+3.6) | 4.0 (+5.2) | .562 (-.050) |
| de-ru | 25.7 (+4.0) | 13.5 (+6.7) | .672 (-.040) |
| es-en | 16.4 (+3.8) | 3.2 (+4.0) | .610 (-.059) |
| es-ru | 20.6 (+4.7) | 8.3 (+6.0) | .643 (-.064) |
| fr-en | 20.5 (+1.5) | 6.0 (+5.8) | .603 (-.031) |
| fr-ru | 21.4 (+6.1) | 15.5 (+10.8) | .704 (-.070) |
| it-en | 15.2 (+3.3) | 3.5 (+2.9) | .663 (-.059) |
| it-ru | 19.6 (+5.5) | 9.4 (+6.7) | .670 (-.071) |
| en-ru | 20.8 (+5.6) | 11.5 (+8.8) | .797 (-.048) |

Table 6: Classification quality of the classifier trained on all features, compared to the baseline trained only on phrase-level features. The relative change of the baseline values is given in brackets.

| Examples | 1700 | 680 | 272 | 108 | 43 |
|---|---|---|---|---|---|
| Accuracy | .803 | .794 | .780 | .757 | .709 |

Table 7: Classification accuracy w.r.t different size of training set averaged over eight language pairs.

We measured the impact of different features, as described in Breiman (2001), with the help of the standard function of the R library "randomForest" (Table 8). The three baseline features were ranked as most important, followed by UnsafeAlign, OOV, UnsafeJump and others.

| Feature | Importance |
|---|---|
| $log(S_{lem})$ | 35.679 |
| $log(P(e\|f))$ | 33.9729 |
| $log(P(f\|e))$ | 28.8637 |
| $UnsafeAlign$ | 24.3705 |
| $OOV$ | 22.8306 |
| $UnsafeJump$ | 20.1108 |
| $Punct$ | 15.4501 |
| $UnsafeStruct$ | 15.1157 |
| $Uniqueness$ | 13.5049 |
| $UnsafeDigAlign$ | 12.915 |

Table 8: Feature importance measured by the mean decrease of classification accuracy (Breiman, 2001). The value is averaged over the nine language pairs.

We explored the dependence of the prediction accuracy on the co-occurrence frequency of a phrase pair for the classifiers trained on the full feature set and on the baseline feature set. The results for German-English and French-English language pairs are shown in Figure 2. The accuracy function was smoothed with cubic smoothing spline. The differences in the distribution of classification errors between language pairs suggest that the nature of the noise can vary for different corpora. The general U shape of the curves in Figure 2 is partly due to the fact that there are many true negatives in the low-frequency area, and many true positives in the high-frequency area.

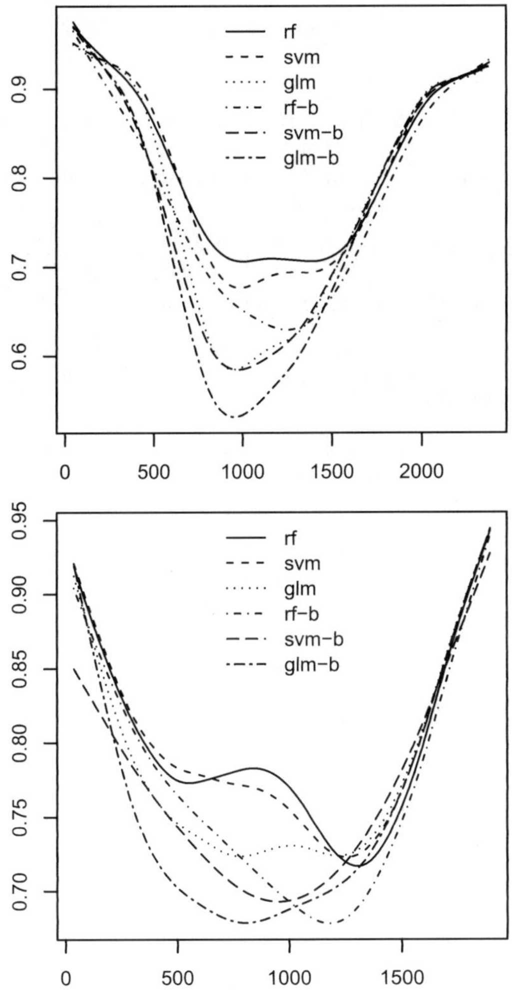


Figure 2: Prediction accuracy of different classifiers w.r.t. the phrase pairs sorted by the ascending co-occurrence count. The upper plot relates to the German-English pair, the bottom relates to French-English pair. The labels rf, svm, glm refer to the classifiers trained on the full feature set; rf-b, svm-b, glm-b refer to the baseline setting.

Table 9 reports the top English translations of the French word "connexion" before the noise reduction and shows which variants were recognized as positive and negative by the RF classifier.

| English | $C(e, f)$ | $p(f\|e)$ | $p(e\|f)$ | RF |
|---|---|---|---|---|
| connection | 58018 | 0.689 | 0.374 | + |
| wireless | 32630 | 0.450 | 0.211 | - |
| free | 31775 | 0.113 | 0.205 | - |
| wifi | 16272 | 0.382 | 0.105 | - |
| login | 4910 | 0.443 | 0.032 | + |
| connectivity | 394 | 0.055 | 0.003 | + |
| logon | 290 | 0.185 | 0.002 | + |
| access | 276 | 0.001 | 0.002 | - |
| link | 148 | 0.001 | 0.001 | - |

Table 9: English translations of the French word "connexion". $C(e, f)$ is the co-occurrence count, $p(f|e)$, $p(e|f)$ are the translation probabilities of lemmatized pairs. The last column shows the classification result.

## 5 Conclusion

The main contributions of this paper are the following. We address the problem of noise reduction in automatic construction of human-oriented translation dictionary. We introduce an approach to increase the precision of automatically acquired bilingual lexicon, which allows to mitigate the negative impact of a noisy corpus. Our noise reduction method relies on the supervised learning on a small set of annotated translation pairs. In addition to the phrase-level statistics, such as co-occurrence counts and translation probabilities, we propose a set of non-lexical context features based on the analysis of sentences in which a phrase pair occurred. The experiment demonstrates a substantial improvement in the accuracy of the detection of noisy translations, compared to a baseline which uses only phrase-level statistics.

We have shown that the proposed noise detection method is applicable to various language pairs. The alignment-based features can be easily obtained for any parallel corpus, even if other tools do not exist. We hope that our noise detection approach can also be adapted for SMT phrase-tables, if the initial parallel sentences are still available.

## References

B. T. Sue Atkins. 1994. *A corpus-based dictionary*. In Oxford-Hachette French Dictionary, Introduction xix-xxxii. Oxford: Oxford University Press.

Leo Breiman. 2001. *Random Forests*. Machine Learning 45 5-32.

Peter F. Brown, Stephen A. Della Pietra, Vincent J. Della Pietra and Robert L. Mercer. 1993. *The Mathematics of Statistical Machine Translation: Parameter estimation*. Computational Linguistics, 19(2):263–312, June.

Matthias Eck, Stephan Vogel, and Alex Waibel. 2007. *Translation model pruning via usage statistics for statistical machine translation*. In Human Language Technologies 2007: The Conference of the NAACL; Companion Volume, Short Papers, pages 21–24, Rochester, New York, April. Association for Computational Linguistics

Pascale Fung. 1998. *A Statistical View on Bilingual Lexicon Extraction from Parallel Corpora to Non-parallel Corpora*. Parallel Text Processing: Alignment and Use of Translation Corpora. Kluwer Academic Publishers

Hartmann, R.R.K. 1994. *The use of parallel text corpora in the generation of translation equivalents for bilingual lexicography*. In W. Martin, et al. (Eds.), Euralex 1994 Proceedings (pp. 291-297). Amsterdam: Vrije Universiteit.

Howard Johnson, Joel Martin, George Foster, and Roland Kuhn 2007. *Improving translation quality by discarding most of the phrasetable*. In Proceedings of EMNLP-CoNLL, ACL, Prague, Czech Republic, pages 967-975.

Philipp Koehn, Franz Josef Och, and Daniel Marcu 2003. *Statistical phrase-based translation*. In Proceedings of HLT-NAACL 2003, pages 127–133.

Philipp Koehn, Hieu Hoang, Alexandra Birch, Chris Callison-Burch, Marcello Federico, Nicola Bertoldi, Brooke Cowan, Wade Shen, Christine Moran, Richard Zens, Chris Dyer, Ondřej Bojar, Alexandra Constantin, and Evan Herbst 2007. *Moses: Open source toolkit for statistical machine translation*. In Proceedings of the 45th Annual Meeting of the ACL on Interactive Poster and Demonstration Sessions, pages 177–180, Prague, Czech Republic

Akira Kumano and Hideki Hirakawa. 1994. *Building An MT Dictionary From Parallel Texts Based On Linguistic And Statistical Information*. COLING 1994: 76-81

Wang Ling, João Graça, Isabel Trancoso and Alan Black 2012. *Entropy-based Pruning for Phrase-based Machine Translation*. In Proceedings of EMNLP-CoNLL, Association for Computational Linguistics, Jeju Island, Korea, pp. 972-983

C. J. A. McEwan, I. Ounis, and I. Ruthven. 2002. *Building bilingual dictionaries from parallel web documents*. In Proceedings of the 24th BCS-IRSG European Colloquium on IR Research, pp. 303-323. Springer-Verlag.

I. Dan Melamed. 1996. *Automatic construction of clean broad-coverage translation lexicons*. In Proceedings of the 2nd Conference of the Association for Machine Translation in the Americas, pages 125–134, Montreal, Canada

I. Dan Melamed. 2000. *Models of Translational Equivalence among Words*. Computational Linguistics 26(2), 221-249, June.

Robert C. Moore. 2004. *On Log-Likelihood-Ratios and the Significance of Rare Events*. In Proceedings of the 2004 Conference on Empirical Methods in Natural Language Processing, Barcelona, Spain.

Franz Josef Och and Hermann Ney. 2000. *Improved Statistical Alignment Models*. Proceedings of the 38th Annual Meeting of the ACL, pp. 440-447, Hongkong, China.

Franz Josef Och and Hermann Ney. 2004. *The Alignment Template Approach to Statistical Machine Translation*. Computational Linguistics, vol. 30 (2004), pp. 417-449.

Pablo Gamallo Otero. 2007. *Learning bilingual lexicons from comparable English and Spanish corpora*. Proceedings of MT Summit XI, pages 191–198.

Reinhard Rapp. 1995. *Identifying word translations in non-parallel texts*. In Proceedings of the ACL 33, 320-322.

Resnik, Philip and Noah A. Smith. 2003. *The web as a parallel corpus.*. Computational Linguistics, 29, pp.349–380

Magnus Sahlgren. 2004. *Automatic Bilingual Lexicon Acquisition Using Random Indexing*. Journal of Natural Language Engineering, Special Issue on Parallel Texts, 11.

Serge Sharoff. 2004. *Harnessing the lawless: using comparable corpora to find translation equivalents*. Journal of Applied Linguistics 1(3), 333-350.

Jason Smith, Herve Saint-Amand, Magdalena Plamada, Philipp Koehn, Chris Callison-Burch and Adam Lopez. 2013. *Dirt Cheap Web-Scale Parallel Text from the Common Crawl*. To appear in Proceedings of ACL 2013.

Dan Tufiş and Ana-Maria Barbu. 2001. *Computational Bilingual Lexicography: Automatic Extraction of Translation Dictionaries*. In International Journal on Science and Technology of Information, Romanian Academy, ISSN 1453-8245, 4/3-4, pp.325-352

Velupillai, Sumithra, Martin Hassel, and Hercules Dalianis. 2008. *"Automatic Dictionary Construction and Identification of Parallel Text Pairs*. In Proceedings of the International Symposium on Using Corpora in Contrastive and Translation Studies (UC-CTS).

Richard Zens, Daisy Stanton and Peng Xu. 2012. *A Systematic Comparison of Phrase Table Pruning Techniques*. In Proceedings of EMNLP-CoNLL, ACL, Jeju Island, Korea, pp. 972-983.

# Adventures in Multilingual Parsing

**Joakim Nivre**
Uppsala university
Department of Linguistics and Philology
Uppsala, Sweden

## 1 Introduction

The typological diversity of the world's languages poses important challenges for the techniques used in machine translation, syntactic parsing and other areas of natural language processing. Statistical models developed and tuned for English do not necessarily perform well for richly inflected languages, where larger morphological paradigms and more flexible word order gives rise to data sparseness. Since paradigms can easily be captured in rule-based descriptions, this suggests that hybrid approaches combining statistical modeling with linguistic descriptions might be more effective. However, in order to gain more insight into the benefits of different techniques from a typological perspective, we also need linguistic resources that are comparable across languages, something that is currently lacking to a large extent.

In this talk, I will report on two ongoing projects that tackle these issues in different ways. In the first part, I will describe techniques for joint morphological and syntactic parsing that combines statistical dependency parsing and rule-based morphological analysis, specifically targeting the challenges posed by richly inflected languages. In the second part, I will present the Universal Dependency Treebank Project, a recent initiative seeking to create multilingual corpora with morphosyntactic annotation that is consistent across languages.

## 2 Morphological and Syntactic Parsing

In Bohnet et al. (2013), the goal is to improve parsing accuracy for morphologically rich languages by performing morphological and syntactic analysis jointly instead of in a pipeline. In this way, we can ideally make use of syntactic information to disambiguate morphology, and not just vice versa. We use a transition-based framework for dependency parsing, and explore different ways of integrating morphological features into the model. Furthermore, we investigate the use of rule-based morphological analyzers to provide hard or soft constraints in order to tackle the sparsity of lexical features. Evaluation on five morphologically rich languages (Czech, Finnish, German, Hungarian, and Russian) shows consistent improvements in both morphological and syntactic accuracy for joint prediction over a pipeline model, with further improvements thanks to the morphological analyzers. The final results improve the state of the art in dependency parsing for all languages.

## 3 Treebanks for Multilingual Parsing

In McDonald et al. (2013), we present a new collection of treebanks with homogeneous syntactic annotation for six languages: German, English, Swedish, Spanish, French and Korean. The annotation is based on the Google universal part-of-speech tags (Petrov et al., 2012) and the Stanford dependencies (de Marneffe et al., 2006), adapted and harmonized across languages. To show the usefulness of such a resource, we also present a case study of cross-lingual transfer parsing with more reliable evaluation than has been possible before. The 'universal' treebank is made freely available in order to facilitate research on multilingual dependency parsing.[1] A second release including eleven languages is planned for the spring of 2014.

## 4 Conclusion

Although both projects reviewed in the talk may contribute to a better understanding of how natural language processing techniques are affected by linguistic diversity, there are still important gaps that need to be filled. For instance, the universal treebank annotation still fails to capture most of the morphological categories used by the parser. In the final part of the talk, I will try to outline some of the challenges that lie ahead of us.

[1] Downloadable at https://code.google.com/p/uni-dep-tb/.

## References


Bernd Bohnet, Joakim Nivre, Igor Boguslavsky, Richárd Farkas, Filip Ginter, and Jan Hajič. 2013. Joint morphological and syntactic analysis for richly inflected languages. *Transactions of the Association for Computational Linguistics*, 1:415–428.

Marie-Catherine de Marneffe, Bill MacCartney, and Christopher D. Manning. 2006. Generating typed dependency parses from phrase structure parses. In *Proceedings of the 5th International Conference on Language Resources and Evaluation (LREC)*.

Ryan McDonald, Joakim Nivre, Yvonne Quirmbach-Brundage, Yoav Goldberg, Dipanjan Das, Kuzman Ganchev, Keith Hall, Slav Petrov, Hao Zhang, Oscar Täckström, Claudia Bedini, Núria Bertomeu Castelló, and Jungmee Lee. 2013. Universal dependency annotation for multilingual parsing. In *Proceedings of the 51st Annual Meeting of the Association for Computational Linguistics (Volume 2: Short Papers)*, pages 92–97.

Slav Petrov, Dipanjan Das, and Ryan McDonald. 2012. A universal part-of-speech tagset. In *Proceedings of the 8th International Conference on Language Resources and Evaluation (LREC)*.

# Machine translation for LSPs: strategy and implementation

**Maxim Khalilov**

bmmt GmbH

Alt-Moabit 92
10559 Berlin
Germany
maxim.khalilov@machine-translation.eu

## Abstract

Over the last few years, machine translation (MT) has transformed from an academic research platform into a productivity or gisting tool adopted by several end users. In this talk, I will describe some of the business and technical MT-related challenges faced by language service providers nowadays. I will describe the approach we take at bmmt GmbH to create innovative industry solutions driven by MT.

# A Principled Approach to Context-Aware Machine Translation

**Rafael E. Banchs**
Institute for Infocomm Research
1 Fusionopolis Way, #21-01, Singapore 138632
rembanchs@i2r.a-star.edu.sg

## Abstract

This paper presents a new principled approach to context-aware machine translation. The proposed approach reformulates the posterior probability of a translation hypothesis given the source input by incorporating the source-context information as an additional conditioning variable. As a result, a new model component, which is referred to as the context-awareness model, is added into the original noisy channel framework. A specific computational implementation for the new model component is also described along with its main properties and limitations.

## 1 Introduction

It is well known that source-context information plays a significant role in human-based language translation (Padilla and Bajo, 1998). A similar claim can be supported for the case of Machine Translation on the grounds of the Distributional Hypothesis (Firth, 1957). According to the Distributional Hypothesis, much of the meaning of a given word is implied by its context rather than by the word itself.

In this work, we first focus our attention on the fact that the classical formulation of the statistical machine translation framework, implicitly disregards the role of source-context information within the translation generation process. Based on this, we propose a principled reformulation that allows for introducing context-awareness into the statistical machine translation framework. Then, a specific computational implementation for the newly proposed model is derived and described, along with its main properties and limitations.

The remainder of the paper is structured as follows. First, in section 2, the theoretical background and motivation for this work are presented. Then, in section 3, the proposed model derivation is described. In section 4, a specific computational implementation for the model is provided. And, finally in section 5, main conclusions and future research work are presented.

## 2 Theoretical Background

According to the original formulation of the translation problem within the statistical framework, the decoding process is implemented by means of a probability maximization mechanism:

$$\hat{T} = \operatorname{argmax}_T \, p(T|S) \qquad (1)$$

which means that the most likely translation $\hat{T}$ for a source sentence $S$ is provided by the hypothesis $T$ that maximizes the conditional probability of $T$ given $S$.

Furthermore, by considering the noisy channel approach introduced in communications theory, the formulation in (1) can be rewritten as:

$$\hat{T} = \operatorname{argmax}_T \, p(S|T)\, p(T) \qquad (2)$$

where the likelihood $p(S|T)$ is referred to as the translation model and the prior $p(T)$ is referred to as the language model.

Notice from the resulting formulation in (2) that, as the maximization runs over the translation hypothesis space $\{T\}$, the evidence $p(S)$ is not accounted for.

This particular consequence of the mathematical representation in (2) is counterintuitive to the notion of source-context information being useful for selecting appropriate translations.

This problem becomes more relevant when the probability models in (2) are decomposed into sub-sentence level probabilities for operational purposes. Indeed, the computational implementation of (2) requires the decomposition of sentence-level probabilities $p(S|T)$ and $p(T)$ into sub-sentence level probabilities $p(s|t)$ and $p(t)$, were $s$ and $t$ refer to sub-sentence units, such as words or groups of words.

In the original problem formulation (Brown et al., 1993), the sentence-level translation model $p(S|T)$ in (2) is approximated by means of word-level probabilities, and the sentence-level language model $p(T)$ is approximated by means of word $n$-gram probabilities.

Within this framework, translation probabilities at the sentence-level are estimated from word-level probabilities as follows[1]:

$$p(S|T) = \prod_k \sum_n p(s_k|t_n) \qquad (3)$$

where $s_k$ and $t_n$ refer to individual words occurring in $S$ and $T$, respectively. The probabilities $p(s_k|t_n)$ are referred to as lexical models and they represent the probability of an individual source word $s_k$ to be the translation of a given target word $t_n$. These lexical models are estimated by using word alignment probabilities.

In statistical phrase-based translation (Koehn et al., 2003), the translation model is approximated by means of phrase-level probabilities (a phrase is a bilingual pair of sub-sentence units that is consistent with the word alignments).

Within this framework, translation probabilities at the sentence-level are computed from phrase-level probabilities as follows:

$$p(S|T) = \prod_i p(s_i|t_i) \qquad (4)$$

where $s_i$ and $t_i$ refer to phrases (i.e. groups of words) occurring in $S$ and $T$, respectively. The probabilities $p(s_i|t_i)$ are estimated by means of relative frequencies and, accordingly, they are referred to as relative frequency models.

Finally, in (Och and Ney, 2002), the maximum entropy framework was introduced into machine translation and the two-model formulation in the noisy channel approach (2) was extended to the log-linear combination of as many relevant models as can be reasonably derived from the training data. In addition, the maximum entropy framework also allows for tuning the weights in the log-linear combinations of models by means of discriminative training.

Within this framework, translation probabilities at the sentence-level are estimated from phrase-level probabilities as follows:

$$p(T|S) = \frac{1}{\zeta}\exp\{\textstyle\sum_i \sum_m \lambda_m\, h_m(t_i, s_i)\} \qquad (5)$$

where $h_m(s_i, t_i)$ are referred to as feature models or functions, $\lambda_m$ are the feature weights of the log-linear combination, and $\zeta$ is a normalization factor. Notice from (5) that in the maximum entropy framework the posterior probability $p(T|S)$ is modeled rather than the likelihood.

[1] For the sake of clarity additional model components such as fertility, reordering and distortion are omitted in both (3) and (4).

From (3) and (4), it is clear that source-context information is not taken into account during translation hypothesis generation. In such cases, the individual sub-sentence unit probabilities depend only on the restricted context provided by the same sub-sentence unit level as observed from the training data.

In the case of (5), on the other hand, some room is left for incorporating source-context information in the hypothesis generation process by means of context-aware feature models. This is basically done by using features that relate the occurrences of sub-sentence units with relevant source-context information of lager extension.

Several research works have already addressed the problem of incorporating source context information into the translation process within the maximum entropy framework (Carpuat and Wu, 2007; Carpuat and Wu 2008; Haque et al. 2009; España-Bonet et al. 2009; Costa-jussà and Banchs 2010; Haque et al. 2010; Banchs and Costa-jussà 2011).

In the following section, we will reformulate the translation problem, as originally described in (1), in order to provide a principled approach to context-aware machine translation for both the noisy channel and the phrase-based approaches. As seen later, this will result in the incorporation of a new model component, which can be also used as a feature function within the context of the maximum entropy framework.

## 3 Model Derivation

In our proposed formulation for context-aware machine translation, we assume that the most likely translation $\hat{T}$ for a source sentence $S$ does not depends on $S$ only, but also on the context $C$ in which $S$ occurs. While this information might be not too relevant when estimating probabilities at the sentence level, it certainly becomes a very useful evidence support at the sub-sentence level.

Based on this simple idea, we can reformulate the mathematical representation of the translation problem presented in (1) as follows:

$$\hat{T} = \text{argmax}_T\, p(T|S, C) \qquad (6)$$

where $p(T|S, C)$ is the conditional probability of a translation hypothesis $T$ given the source sentence $S$ and the context $C$ in which $S$ occurs. This means that the most likely translation $\hat{T}$ for a source sentence $S$ is provided by the hypothesis $T$ that maximizes the conditional probability of $T$ given $S$ and $C$.

For now, let us just consider the context to be any unit of source language information with larger span than the one of the units used to represent $S$. For instance, if $S$ is a sentence, $C$ can be either a paragraph or a full document; if $S$ is a sub-sentence unit, $C$ can be a sentence; and so on.

From the theoretical point of view, the formulation in (6) is supported by the assumptions of the Distributional Hypothesis, which states that meaning is mainly derived from context rather than from individual language units. According to this, the formulation in (6) allows for incorporating context information into the translation generation process, in a similar way humans take source-context information into account when producing a translation.

After some mathematical manipulations, the conditional probability in (6) can be rewritten as follows:

$$p(T|S,C) = \frac{p(C|S,T)\, p(S|T)\, p(T)}{p(C|S)\, p(S)} \qquad (7)$$

where $p(S|T)$ and $p(T)$ are the same translation and language model probabilities as in (2), and $p(C|S,T)$ is the conditional probability of the source-context $C$ given the translation pair $\langle S,T \rangle$.

Notice that if the translation pair is independent of the context, i.e. $\langle S,T \rangle \perp C$, then (7) reduces to:

$$p(T|S,C) = \frac{p(S|T)\, p(T)}{p(S)} \qquad (8)$$

and the context-aware formulation in (6) reduces to the noisy channel formulation presented earlier in (2).

If we assume, on the other hand, that the translation pair is not independent of the context, the formulation in (6) can be rewritten in terms of (7) as follows:

$$\hat{T} = \text{argmax}_T\, p(C|S,T)\, p(S|T)\, p(T) \qquad (9)$$

As seen from (2) and (9), the proposed context-aware machine translation formulation is similar to the noisy channel approach formulation with the difference that a new probability model has been introduced: $p(C|S,T)$. This new model will be referred to as the context-awareness model, and it acts as a complementary model, which favors those translation hypotheses $T$ for which the current source context $C$ is highly probable given the translation pair $\langle S,T \rangle$.

In the same way translation probabilities $p(S|T)$ at the sentence-level can be estimated from lower-level unit probabilities, such as word or phrases, context-awareness probabilities at the sentence-level can be also estimated from lower-level unit probabilities. For instance, $p(C|S,T)$ can be approximated by means of phrase-level probabilities according to the following equation:

$$p(C|S,T) = \prod_i p(C|s_i,t_i) \qquad (10)$$

where $s_i$ and $t_i$ refer to phrase pairs occurring in $S$ and $T$, respectively, and $C$ is the source-context for the translation under consideration.

In the following section we develop a specific computational implementation for estimating the probabilities of the context-awareness model.

## 4 Model Implementation

Before developing a specific implementation for the context-awareness model in (10), we need to define what type of units $s_i$ and $t_i$ will be used and what kind of source-context information $C$ will be taken into account.

Here, we will consider the phrase-based machine translation scenario, where phrase pairs $<s_i,t_i>$ are used as the building blocks of the translation generation process. Accordingly, and in order to be relevant, the span of the context information to be used must be larger than the one implicitly accounted for by the phrases.

Typically, phrases span vary from one to several words, but most of the time they remain within the sub-sentence level. Then, a context definition at the sentence-level should be appropriate for the purpose of estimating context-awareness probabilities at the phrase-level. In this way, we can consider the context evidence $C$ to be the same sentence being translated $S$.

With these definitions on place, we can now propose a maximum likelihood approach for estimating context-awareness probabilities at the phrase-level. According to this, the probabilities can be computed by using relative frequencies as follows:

$$p(S|s_i,t_i) = \frac{count\ (S,s_i,t_i)}{count\ (s_i,t_i)} \qquad (11)$$

where the numerator accounts for the number of times the phrase pair $<s_i,t_i>$ has been seen along with context $S$ in the training data, and the denominator accounts for the number of times the phrase pair $<s_i,t_i>$ has been seen along with any context in the training data.

While the computation of the denominator in (11) is trivial, i.e. it just needs to count the number of times <$s_i, t_i$> occurs in the parallel text, the computation of the numerator requires certain consideration.

Indeed, if we consider the context to be the source sentence being translated $S$, counting the number of times a phrase pair <$s_i, t_i$> has been seen along with context $S$ implies that $S$ is expected to appear several times in the training data. In practice, this rarely occurs! According to this, the counts for the numerator in (11) will be zero most of the time (when the sentence being translated is not contained in the training data) or, eventually, one (when the sentence being translated is contained in the training data).

Moreover, if the sentence being translated is contained in the training data, then its translation is already known! So, why do we need to generate any translation at all?

To circumvent this apparent inconsistency of the model, and to compute proper estimates for the values of $count\ (S, s_i, t_i)$, our proposed model implementation uses fractional counts. This means that, instead of considering integer counts of exact occurrences of the context $S$ within the training data, we will consider fractional counts to account for the occurrences of contexts that are similar to $S$. In order to serve this purpose, a similarity metric within the range from zero (no similarity at all) to one (maximum similarity) is required.

In this way, for each source sentence $S_{i,k}$ in the training data that is associated to the phrase pair <$s_i, t_i$>, its corresponding fractional count would be given by the similarity between $S_{i,k}$ and the input sentence being translated $S$.

$$fcount(S_{i,k}) = sim(S, S_{i,k}) \qquad (12)$$

According to this, the numerator in (11) can be expressed in terms of (12) as:

$$count\ (S, s_i, t_i) = \sum_k sim(S, S_{i,k}) \qquad (13)$$

and the context-awareness probability estimates can be computed as:

$$p(S|s_i, t_i) = \frac{\sum_k sim(S, S_{i,k})}{\sum_k sim(S_{i,k}, S_{i,k})} \qquad (14)$$

Notice that in (14) it is assumed that the number of times the phrase pair <$s_i, t_i$> occurs in the parallel text, i.e. $count\ (s_i, t_i)$, is equal to the number of sentence pairs containing <$s_i, t_i$>. In other words, multiple occurrences of the same phrase pair within a bilingual sentence pair are accounted for only once.

Finally, two important differences between the context-awareness model presented here and other conventional models used in statistical machine translation must be highlighted.

First, notice that the context-awareness model is a dynamic model, in the sense that it has to be estimated at run-time. In fact, as the model probabilities depend on the input sentence to be translated, such probabilities cannot be computed beforehand as in the case of other models.

Second, different from the lexical models and relative frequencies that can be computed on both directions (source-to-target and target-to-source), a symmetric version of the context-awareness model cannot be implemented for decoding. This is basically because estimating probabilities of the form $p(T|s_i, t_i)$ requires the knowledge of the translation output $T$, which is not known until decoding is completed.

However, the symmetric version of the context-awareness model can be certainly used at a post-processing stage, such as in *n*-best rescoring; or, alternatively, an incremental implementation can be devised for its use during decoding.

## 5 Conclusions and Future Work

We have presented a new principled approach to context-aware machine translation. The proposed approach reformulates the posterior probability of a translation hypothesis given the source input by incorporating the source-context information as and additional conditioning variable. As a result, a new probability model component, the context-awareness model, has been introduced into the noisy channel approach formulation.

We also presented a specific computational implementation of the context-awareness model, in which likelihoods are estimated for the context evidence at the phrase-level based on the use of fractional counts, which can be computed by means of a similarity metric.

Future work in this area includes efficient run-time implementations and comparative evaluations of different similarity metrics to be used for computing the fractional counts. Similarly, a comparative evaluation between an incremental implementation of the symmetric version of the context-awareness model and its use in a post-processing stage should be also conducted.

**Acknowledgments**

The author wants to thank $I^2R$ for its support and permission to publish this work, as well as the reviewers for their insightful comments.

## References


Banchs, R.E., Costa-jussà, M. R. 2011. A Semantic Feature for Statistical Machine Translation. In Proceedings of the Fifth Workshop on Syntax, Semantics and Structure in Statistical Translation, ACL HLT 2011, pp. 126-134.

Brown, P., Della-Pietra, S., Della-Pietra, V., Mercer, R. 1993. The Mathematics of Statistical Machine Translation: Computational Linguistics 19(2), 263--311

Carpuat, M., Wu, D. 2007. How Phrase Sense Disambiguation Outperforms Word Sense Disambiguation for Statistical Machine Translation. In: 11th International Conference on Theoretical and Methodological Issues in Machine Translation. Skovde

Carpuat, M., Wu, D. 2008. Evaluation of Context-Dependent Phrasal Translation Lexicons for Statistical Machine Translation. In: 6th International Conference on Language Resources and Evaluation (LREC). Marrakech

Costa-jussà, M. R., Banchs, R.E. 2010. A Vector-Space Dynamic Feature for Phrase-Based Statistical Machine Translation. Journal of Intelligent Information Systems

España-Bonet, C., Gimenez, J., Marquez, L. 2009. Discriminative Phrase-Based Models for Arabic Machine Translation. ACM Transactions on Asian Language Information Processing Journal (Special Issue on Arabic Natural Language Processing)

Firth, J.R. 1957. A synopsis of linguistic theory 1930-1955. Studies in linguistic analysis, 51: 1-31

Haque, R., Naskar, S. K., Ma, Y., Way, A. 2009. Using Supertags as Source Language Context in SMT. In: 13th Annual Conference of the European Association for Machine Translation, pp. 234--241. Barcelona

Haque, R., Naskar, S. K., van den Bosh, A., Way, A. 2010. Supertags as Source Language Context in Hierarchical Phrase-Based SMT. In: 9th Conference of the Association for Machine Translation in the Americas (AMTA)

Koehn, P., Och, F. J., Marcu, D. 2003. Statistical Phrase-Based Translation. In: Human Language Technology Conference and Conference on Empirical Methods in Natural Language Processing (HLTEMNLP), pp. 48--54. Edmonton

Och, F. J., Ney, H. (2002) Discriminative Training and Maximum Entropy Models for Statistical Machine Translation. In: 40th Annual Meeting of the Association for Computational Linguistics, pp. 295--302

Padilla, P., Bajo, T. (1998) Hacia un Modelo de Memoria y Atención en la Interpretación Simultánea. Quaderns: Revista de Traducció 2, 107--117

# Deriving *de/het* gender classification for Dutch nouns for rule-based MT generation tasks

**Bogdan Babych**
Centre for Translation Studies
University of Leeds
b.babych@leeds.ac.uk

**Jonathan Geiger**
Lingenio GmbH
geiger@cl.uni-heidelberg.de

**Mireia Ginestí Rosell**
Centre for Translation Studies
University of Leeds
mireia.ginesti@gmail.com

**Kurt Eberle**
Lingenio GmbH
k.eberle@lingenio.de

## Abstract

Linguistic resources available in the public domain, such as lemmatisers, part-of-speech taggers and parsers can be used for the development of MT systems: as separate processing modules or as annotation tools for the training corpus. For SMT this annotation is used for training factored models, and for the rule-based systems linguistically annotated corpus is the basis for creating analysis, generation and transfer dictionaries from corpora. However, the annotation in many cases is insufficient for rule-based MT, especially for the generation tasks. In this paper we analyze a specific case when the part-of-speech tagger does not provide information about de/het gender of Dutch nouns that is needed for our rule-based MT systems translating into Dutch. We show that this information can be derived from large annotated monolingual corpora using a set of context-checking rules on the basis of co-occurrence of nouns and determiners in certain morphosyntactic configurations. As not all contexts are sufficient for disambiguation, we evaluate the coverage and the accuracy of our method for different frequency thresholds in the news corpora. Further we discuss possible generalization of our method, and using it to automatically derive other types of linguistic information needed for rule-based MT: syntactic subcategorization frames, feature agreement rules and contextually appropriate collocates.



## 1 Introduction

This paper evaluates a methodology for deriving gender classification of nouns based on their contextual features and light-weight linguistic annotation of a corpus. We approach the problem as reconstructing an enriched set of linguistic features for RBMT generation lexicon from combining implicit information available in corpora with a set of general linguistic principles implemented as a small set of simple hand-crafted contextual rules.

These rules are specified as configurations of part-of-speech codes and operate over configurations of part-of-speech codes designed to capture certain disambiguating linguistic constructions. Theoretically, the rules can be made highly-accurate if the list of disambiguating constructions is exhaustive, but there is a well-known trade-off between Precision, Recall and the development effort for hand-crafted sets of rules. Additional factors to be taken into account are the quality and size of the annotated corpus. In our experiment we take a practical approach, using a minimal set of contextual rules that cover most typical constructions.

We evaluate Precision and coverage for this set of rules for different frequency thresholds of nouns in the corpus. The results indicate the potential of the proposed methodology for a larger set of similar tasks, where we intend to enrich linguistic resources for rule-based MT tasks using implicit linguistic information, which can be discovered in annotated corpora.

The paper is organised as follows: Section 2 discusses linguistic aspects of the gender disambiguation task for Dutch nouns; Section 3 describes the set-up of our experiment on automatically deriving the lexicon for Dutch nouns enriched with gender information; Section 4 presents evaluation results for Precision and coverage for different frequency thresholds; Section 4 gives interpretation of the results; Section 6 discusses the development context, generalisation of our methodology for rule-based MT and some ideas for future work.

## 2 Linguistic aspects of gender disambiguation task for Dutch nouns

Predicting gender of Dutch nouns from their context is a simple and clearly defined contextual disambiguation task, and we can evaluate three aspects of the performance of our method: (a) what coverage and accuracy can be achieved on this task compared to the gold standard; (b) how do the coverage and accuracy change in different frequency thresholds; (c) what is the proportion of contexts which can be used for disambiguation in different frequency thresholds (since some contexts will not disambiguate the features of interest).

Nouns in Dutch belong to one of the two gender classes which determine the choice of the definite articles (used with singular nouns) and other determiners: neuter nouns take determiners *het, dat, dit, ons*, and nouns with the common gender, which historically is the merged masculine and feminine, take *de, die, deze, onze*. Nouns can only be disambiguated when used as singular and take a definite determiner, so not all contexts in corpus which contain nouns can be useful for disambiguation.

The information about *het/de* classification for nouns is a non-interpretable (in terms of the generative grammar) system-internal morphological feature: it characterises only combinatorial properties of nouns, but does not directly influence their syntactic functions in a structure of a sentence or their semantic interpretation (unlike the part-of-speech/Noun category, morphological case and number). Therefore, this feature is much more useful for text generation than for analysis, and belongs to the family of other similar system-internal features, like inflection classes, subcategorisation frames, lexical functions (collocational restrictions), etc. Interestingly, this feature normally operates in the local context of several words within a limited number of possible part-of-speech sequences.

For machine translation task this information needs to be supplied by the target language generation rules, or by the target language model, since it is normally not present in the source text, and cannot be derived from application of transfer rules or the translation model.

There are several wide-coverage part-of-speech taggers and lemmatisers for Dutch in the public domain (open source and/or freely available), such as Dutch parameter files for the TreeTagger (Schmid, 1994), TiMBL / Frog tagger / lemmatiser / dependency parser (Van den Bosch et al., 2007), Alpino system (Bouma et al., 2001). Some of them provide only plain high-level annotation of part-of-speech codes, without gender information for nouns. However, some do generate enriched part-of-speech codes for nouns specifying their gender. Because of this we can benchmark our methodology using this enriched information as gold-standard and calculate Precision in addition to coverage.

## 3 Set-up of the experiment

In our experiment TiMBL / Frog was used to automatically annotate a 60-million-word section of the balanced Dutch SoNaR corpus (Oostdijk et al., 2008).

TiMBL/Frog provides gold-standard dictionary-based information about these classes for identified lemmas. For the prediction task we ignored the gold-standard gender class information, and used only the generic part-of-speech information and the number category for nouns. In the evaluation stage, we compared these automatically predicted gender classes with the gold-standard classes.

Prediction of the *de/het* classes was performed by a set of regular expressions, which cover most typical contexts, where these determiners are distinguished. If both types of determiners were found in different contexts for the same noun, then the class that has the majority of contexts was assigned. Regular expressions covered simple contexts, e.g.: *Det (Adj)? Noun*:

| Frq threshold | Gold standard | Predicted | Wrong | %:100 | Correct | %:100 | Missed | %:100 | Contexts | %:100 |
|---|---|---|---|---|---|---|---|---|---|---|
| *None* | 157066 | 74505 | 2417 | *0.032* | 72088 | *0.968* | 84978 | 0.541 | | *0.752* |
| *Frq>1* | 70006 | 45710 | 1604 | *0.035* | 44106 | *0.965* | 25900 | 0.37 | | *0.573* |
| *Frq>2* | 48002 | 35766 | 1229 | *0.034* | 34537 | *0.966* | 13465 | 0.281 | | *0.518* |
| *Frq>3* | 38084 | 30245 | 1012 | *0.033* | 29233 | *0.967* | 8851 | 0.232 | | *0.491* |
| *Frq>4* | 32051 | 26515 | 858 | *0.032* | 25657 | *0.968* | 6394 | 0.199 | | *0.475* |
| *Frq>5* | 28025 | 23818 | 744 | *0.031* | 23074 | *0.969* | 4951 | 0.177 | | *0.465* |
| *Frq>6* | 25026 | 21735 | 661 | *0.03* | 21074 | *0.97* | 3952 | 0.158 | | *0.456* |
| *Frq>7* | 22789 | 20053 | 597 | *0.03* | 19456 | *0.97* | 3333 | 0.146 | | *0.450* |
| *Frq>8* | 21002 | 18701 | 543 | *0.029* | 18158 | *0.971* | 2844 | 0.135 | | *0.444* |
| *Frq>9* | 19546 | 17553 | 498 | *0.028* | 17055 | *0.972* | 2491 | 0.127 | | *0.440* |
| ... | | | | | | | | | | |
| *Frq>=20* | 12244 | 11436 | 279 | *0.024* | 11157 | *0.976* | 1087 | 0.089 | | *0.421* |
| *Frq>=50* | 6795 | 6482 | 123 | *0.019* | 6359 | *0.981* | 436 | 0.064 | | *0.410* |
| *Frq>=100* | 4297 | 4116 | 69 | *0.017* | 4047 | *0.983* | 250 | 0.058 | | *0.401* |

Table 1. Evaluation of the task of predicting Dutch determiner classes: Number of tokens and proportions in each frequency threshold

*(1) de nieuwe geschiedschrijving*
*the.Gend:COM new history.Gend:COM*

-- but not more complex ambiguous contexts, e.g., sequences of nominal compounds:

*(2) waar is de apparaat-code van mijn kamera?*
*Where is the~Gend:COM device~Gend:NEUT – code~Gend:COM of my camera?*

or cases where *het* is not a determiner, but is mistagged as such: we assumed that such contexts are less frequent and error rate will be limited, so we can save the development effort for our hand-crafted rule set relying on the signal being stronger than noise introduced by such complex cases.

The results reported in this paper were generated using the following two multilevel regular expressions (expressions which operate on the levels of lemmas and parts-of-speech:

```
de/det__art        /(adj|conjcoord)*
(.*)/nounsg

het/det__art       /(adj|conjcoord)*
(.*)/nounsg
```

These regular expressions describe configurations that allow several optional adjectives or coordinative conjunctions between the definite determiner and a singular noun. The noun is captured if the configuration matches the piece of text and classified according to the type of the determiner.

## 4 Evaluation results

The results are presented in Table 1 and Charts 1 and 2, which visualise some of the data from Table 1.

Rows in Table 1 represent different frequency cut-off points, e.g: *None* = no frequency cut-off, *Frq>1* = noun types with frequency greater than one, etc. Columns represent:

- **Gold standard**: the number of noun *types* identified in the gold-standard above the specified frequency
- **Predicted**: the number of noun *types* for which prediction of the gender on the basis of the context in the corpus was made (for the rest prediction was not possible since no disambiguating contexts were found for those noun types)
- **Wrong, %/100**: the number and the proportion of wrongly predicted noun types (of the total number of ***Predicted*** types)

- **Correct, %/100**: the number and the proportion of correctly predicted noun types (of the total number of ***Predicted*** types)
- **Missed, %/100**: the number and the proportion of noun types where prediction of gender was not possible (of the total number of nouns in the ***Gold standard***).
- **Contexts, %/100**: the proportion of contexts for noun *tokens*, which were useful for disambiguation

For instance, the first row shows the figures when no frequency cut-off is applied, e.g.: there were 157066 types labeled as Nouns in our section of SoNaR corpus, of which 74505 Nouns were found in a specific context with a definite determiner that allowed to disambiguate gender. Out of these, 2417 types (3.2%) were disambiguated wrongly for different reasons, 72088 types (96.8%) were disambiguated correctly. However, there still remain 84978 noun types (or 54.1% of the total number of 157066 in the gold standard), which were not disambiguated. In total, in the corpus 75.2% of contexts were useful for de/het disambiguation (contained a definite determiner in the immediate left context, or in a one-word-apart position, being separated by an adjective).

The second row in Table 1 presents the subset of 70006 noun types out of the results presented in the first row for 157066 noun types, i.e., the results only for nouns with frequency more than one; the third row – for noun types with frequencies more than two, etc. The intuition is that prediction for more frequent nouns should be more accurate since more *token* contexts become available for disambiguation of a specific noun *type*.

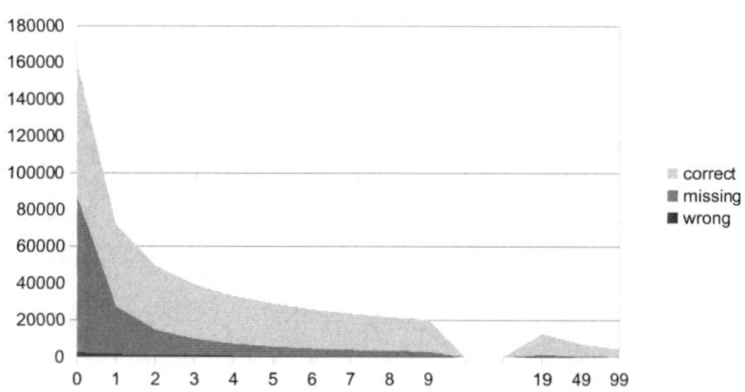


Chart 1. Distribution of correctly predicted, missed and wrongly predicted nouns

Chart 1 visualizes *correct, missing* and *wrong* proportion of noun types in the total count of these types for different frequency cut-off points. On the vertical axis there is a number of noun types, on the horizontal axis – *not greater than* frequencies.

It can be seen from the chart that the proportion of non-disambiguated noun types declines with increasing frequency threshold.

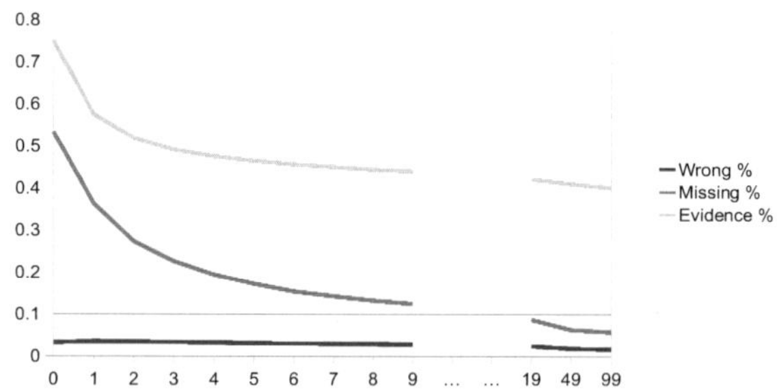


Chart 2. Proportion of context useful for disambiguation (evidence), not predicted (missing) and wrongly predicted (wrong) de/het classes for nouns.

Chart 2 examines the relation between frequency cut-off points and Evidence (top yellow/light line) – the proportions of contexts available for disambiguation; Missing (middle red/medium line) – the proportion of nouns where de/het disambiguation was not possible and Wrong (bottom blue/dark line) – the error rate.

## 5 Interpretation of the results

The following conclusions can be derived from the evaluation data:

1. The Precision even for simple contextual disambiguation rules is surprisingly high: 96.8% for nouns where the prediction was possible. This indicates that simple disambiguation patterns are sufficiently frequent to outweigh more complex patterns which were not covered by the rule and may have lead to errors.
2. For the whole data set (without frequency cut-off) the Recall is much lower: automatic prediction procedure missed 54% of noun tokens that were found in the corpus and a contained

gold-standard gender class, since no disambiguation context was found for these nouns in corpus. However, since more frequent nouns have more chances of occurring in a disambiguation context, mostly low frequent nouns are missed: if we exclude nouns which occurred only once, the procedure misses 37% of nouns; in frequency threshold Frq> 2 it misses even less – 28%, etc.

3. Error rate (proportion of wrongly disambiguated nouns) is relatively stable (3.2% on the whole data set), and does not depend too much on the frequency of nouns: it declines very slowly when the frequency increases (much slower that the coverage of the certain threshold).
4. The proportion of contexts which are useful for disambiguation declines slowly with the increase in frequency threshold, but stabilises around 40% for highly frequent nouns. Interestingly, when the proportion of such contexts goes down, the error rate stays the same.

In general, the results indicate that for practical purposes of rule-based MT development – a sufficiently large list of gender-disambiguated Dutch nouns (around 75000) can be successfully collected from a medium-size corpus (60MW) with very high Precision (96.8%). The method will provide gender disambiguation information for around 46% of all nouns found in the corpus; and for higher frequency threshold the percentage of gender-disambiguated nouns goes up rapidly, flattening at around 90% for Frq>10. This performance reaches the quality standards for creating wide-coverage generation dictionaries for rule-based MT.

## 6 Development context and generalization of the methodology

The task of predicting gender classes for nouns gives indication how other types of similar morphosyntactic resources and representations can be developed and enhanced.

Our methodology is part of a larger development infrastructure for creating a corpus-based development environment for industry-standard rule-based MT systems enhanced with statistical tools and data. The infrastructure uses large monolingual corpora annotated by openly available part-of-speech taggers and lemmatisers, and semi-automatically derives a set of morphological and syntactic patterns for the lexical items found there. These patterns represent advanced linguistic features for the lexicon, such as classification by inflectional morphological paradigms, derivational classes (e.g., gender for nouns), lexical valencies (subcategorisation and case frames), attachment preferences and lexical collocates.

For individual lexical items these patterns do not need to be fully specified from the training corpus: missing forms are reconstructed on the basis of evidence from other lexemes that fit the same pattern, so the system recognises and generates correct output also for unseen forms.

In the context of our hybrid MT development infrastructure this approach particularly targets creation of linguistically-rich resources that generate correct target language forms and phrases. The generation aspect is usually not covered by the annotation tools available in the public domain, so parsers, part-of-speech taggers and lemmatisers usually work only in the direction of analysis, and do not deal with generation).

In a more general context the described infrastructure develops lexical and morphosyntactic resources in a systematic way, so they can be used in a wider range of applications and tasks. It also attempts to bridge the gap between rule-based and statistical techniques in MT by creating rich and highly accurate linguistic representations using corpus-based statistical techniques and integrating them within processing models for hybrid MT architecture.

The central principle of the proposed infrastructure is that advanced morphosyntactic features and representations are derived from corpora annotated with light-weight linguistic features.

The interpretation of this principle is that the tools like part-of-speech taggers and lemmatisers implement a unidirectional *functional perspective* on the morphosyntactic system, which only partially covers the network of linguistic relations involved in the analysis and generation aspects of the language. Rule-based MT application instead need to rely on the alternative *relational perspective* of morphosyntactic representations. Our infrastructure aims at reconstructing this perspective by combining large corpora and unidirectional annotation tools. It derives a range of generation-oriented morphosyntactic features and representations using local context and standard analysis-oriented annotation features in corpora.

The main motivation is that from the point of view of rule-based MT there is a certain imbalance between resources for analysis and annotation of texts on the one hand, and resources for language generation on the other hand. Text annotation resources, such as part-of-speech taggers, lemmatisers, parsers, chunkers – have a longer history of research and development, e.g., (Greene and Rubin, 1971), have created common standards and are more widely available in the public domain, e.g., (Schmid, 1994; Brants, 2000). In their existing form they can be applied to new languages and are more widely used in practical applications. On the other hand, generation-oriented tools are much less accessible, often propitiatory, and lack common standards and shared frameworks for integration of new languages. The predominant unidirectional text-annotation focus might be explained by a historic reason that text annotation was seen as an interesting computational problem with a clearly defined evaluation procedure, which was much harder to develop for the generation tasks.

The idea behind the infrastructure is that if at least some unidirectional annotation tools are available for a certain language, the relational morphosyntactic resources can be automatically developed from large annotated corpora. This will include automatic acquisition of inflectional paradigms for lexical items, attachment preference detection, automatic acquisition of lexical functions. Our infrastructure aims at developing standards and building openly available resources for a number of languages, including under-resourced languages, such as Portuguese, Russian and Ukrainian, in order to carry out the following morphosyntacitc tasks:

1. word form generation: for a given lemma, part-of-speech and inflectional feature values to generate the correct word form, e.g.: *drive~V + Person($3^{rd}$); Number(singular) → drives*
2. generation of paradigms: for a given lemma and part-of-speech to generate a set of all word forms and their inflectional feature values, e.g., *drive~*V → *drive~VV; drives~VVZ; driving~VVG; drove~VVD; driven~VVN*
3. feature agreement generation: for a given sequence of lemmas with their part-of-speech codes to generate a correct sequence of inflected word forms, where inflectional features, e.g., in a language with adjectives and nouns marked for gender to generate a correct gender agreement between the two: in Spanish, e.g., *nuestro~A.Gender(_).Number(_) En:'our' + profesora~N.Gender(fem).Number(plur) En:'professors(female)' → nuestras profesoras*
4. lexical feature generation: to select correct lemmas for lexically underspecified structures, e.g., in a language with the gender feature marked on determiners and nouns to select the correct determiner to go with a given noun: Dutch: *[Determiner.Def(definite)] + beroep~N.Number(singular) → het beroep*
5. subcategorisation frame generation: to generate the correct prepositional phrase and/or morphological case features for a given verb and a noun (or a noun phrase), e.g.: *dispence~V + N → dispense with + N; dispose~V + N → dispose of +N*
6. collocate / lexical function generation (in terms of Mel'čuk, 1998): to select the correct lemma or ranked set of lemmas for a given word and semantic features of its context, e.g., '[not-real/true] + [Noun]': *mock trial; false assumption; counterfeit goods; fake name*
7. word order generation: to generate correct linear sequence of words for a given dependency structure, e.g.:

*I ← find → issues → certain*
*↘ difficult*
➔
*I find certain issues difficult*

The first two functions are performed on internal features of a word, while the other five require contextual input in addition. The described functionality has applications for rule-based MT and Natural Language Generation, which could both benefit from shared standards and the infrastructure of relation-oriented linguistic resources.

## Acknowledgement

The work is supported by the FP7 Marie Curie IAPP project HyghTra: A Hybrid High Quality Translation System, grant agreement no 251534.

## References


Bouma, G., van Noord, G., and R. Malouf. (2001). Alpino: wide coverage computational analysis of Dutch. In W. Daelemans, K. Sima'an, J. Veenstra, and J. Zavrel, editors, Computational Linguistics in the Netherlands 2000, pages 45--59. Rodolpi, Amsterdam.

Brants, T. (2000), TnT - A Statistical Part-of-Speech Tagger. In Proceedings of the Sixth Applied Natural Language Processing Conference ANLP-2000, Seattle, WA.

Greene, B. B. & Rubin, G. M. (1971), Automatic Grammatical Tagging of English. Department of Linguistics, Brown University, Providence, Rhode Island

Mel'čuk, I. A. (1998). Collocations and Lexical Functions. In Anthony P. Cowie (ed.) Phraseology. Theory, analysis, and applications, 23–53. Oxford: Clarendon.

Oostdijk, N., M. Reynaert, P. Monachesi, G. van Noord, R. Ordelman, I. Schuurman, V. Vandeghinste. From D-Coi to SoNaR: A reference corpus for Dutch. In: LREC 2008.

Schmid, H. (1994), Probabilistic Part-of-Speech Tagging Using Decision Trees. Proceedings of International Conference on New Methods in Language Processing, Manchester, UK.

Van den Bosch, A., Busser, G.J., Daelemans, W., and Canisius, S. (2007). An efficient memory-based morphosyntactic tagger and parser for Dutch, In F. van Eynde, P. Dirix, I. Schuurman, and V. Vandeghinste (Eds.), Selected Papers of the 17th Computational Linguistics in the Netherlands Meeting, Leuven, Belgium, pp. 99-114.

# Chinese-to-Spanish rule-based machine translation system

**Jordi Centelles**[1] **and Marta R. Costa-jussà**[2]
[1]Centre de Tecnologies i Aplicacions del llenguatge i la Parla (TALP),
Universitat Politècnica de Catalunya (UPC), Barcelona
[2]Centro de Investigación en Computación (CIC), Instituto Politécnico Nacional (IPN), Mexico
[1]jordi.centelles.sabater@alu-etsetb.upc.edu, [2]marta@nlp.cic.ipn.mx

## Abstract

This paper describes the first freely available Chinese-to-Spanish rule-based machine translation system. The system has been built using the Apertium technology and combining manual and statistical techniques. Evaluation in different test sets shows a high coverage between 82-88%.

## 1 Introduction

Chinese and Spanish are two of the most spoken languages in the world and they are gaining interest in the actual information society. In this sense, machine translation (MT) between these two languages would be clearly of interest for companies, tourists, students and politicians. Eventhough the necessity is a fact, there are not many Chinese-to-Spanish MT systems available in the Internet. In addition, the translation quality is quite behind the standards. Most of the approaches are corpus-based and they seem to produce translation through English pivoting to compensate the lack of Chinese-Spanish parallel corpora.

When it comes to academic research, there have been few works in these pair of languages which mainly are reviewed in Costa-jussà et al (2012b) and they also rely on the pivoting procedure. The linguistic differences (mainly at the level of morphology) between the two languages makes the training of data-driven systems rather difficult. Actually, Chinese and Spanish are languages with many linguistic differences, especially at the level of morphology and semantics. Chinese is an isolating language, which means that there is a one-to-one correspondence between words and morphemes. Whereas, Spanish is a fusional language, which means that words and morphemes are mixed together without clear limits. Regarding semantics, Chinese is a language that has a massive number of homophonyms at the lexical level (Zhang et al., 2006). Therefore, lexical semantic disambiguation towards Spanish will be harder.

Given these challenges, we decided to build a Chinese-to-Spanish rule-based machine translation (RBMT) system. These types of systems provide a translation based on linguistic knowledge in contrast to the existing and popular corpus-based approaches. The translation process is divided in: analysis, transfer and generation. Analysis and generation cover mainly the morphological and semantic variations of the languages, the transfer phase is in charge of the grammatical aspects (Hutchins and Sommers, 1992). The main advantages of RBMT are that they use linguistic knowledge and the produced errors can be traced.

Among the different linguistic motivations to build a Chinese-to-Spanish RBMT, we can list the following: (1) the proposed system will coherently manage the difference in morphology from Chinese to Spanish; (2) and the RBMT approach is able to exploit the use of linguistic tools which are available separately for Chinese and Spanish.

The main drawback of a RBMT system is that it requires a lot of human dedication and years of development (Costa-Jussà et al., 2012a) and that they exhibit weakness in lexical selection transfer, which is quite relevant in this pair of languages. However, in our case, we are using the Apertium platform (Forcada et al., 2011) that eases the process. In addition, when building the proposed RBMT approach, we use automatic techniques to feed the system from parallel corpus.

The rest of the paper is organized as follows. Section 2 reports a detailed description of the Chinese-to-Spanish RBMT architecture including the procedure of compiling monolingual and bilingual dictionaries as well as the computation of grammatical transfer rules. Section 3 reports an evaluation of the system in terms of coverage. Finally, Section 4 discusses the results and it draws the final conclusions.

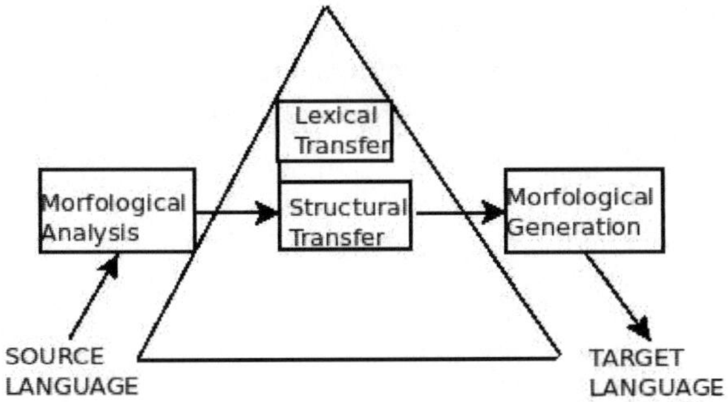


Figure 1: Block diagram of a typical rule-based machine translation system.

## 2 Rule-based machine translation architecture

The general architecture of a RBMT translation architecture has been defined in the literature in works such as (Hutchins and Sommers, 1992) or (Forcada et al., 2011), which is the open-source toolbox that we are using in this paper. In this section, we describe in detail how the system has been developed following similar procedures as (Cortés et al., 2012). Novelties in our work are that we are aiming a really challenging language pair with few bilingual speakers capable of developing the resources required to compile the targeted system.

Human annotation counted with two bilingual English-Spanish annotators and one trilingual annotator Chinese-English-Spanish, who was in charge of checking every step out.

### 2.1 System architecture

The system is based on the Apertium platform (Forcada et al., 2011) which is a free/open-source toolbox for shallow transfer machine translation. As well as the platform, the linguistic data for the MT systems are also available under the terms of the GNU GPL.

The platform was originally designed for the Romance languages of Spain, but it is moving away from those initial objectives (see the list of available languages in *wiki.apertium.org*. In practice, we use the architecture of the system, but, differently, we are using statistical techniques to complete our system.

Figure 1 shows the representative block diagram modules of the RBMT system. In this first description of the system, the only step that is not addressed is the lexical transfer.

Development to date has consisted of: feeding monolingual and bilingual dictionaries, to extend coverage, with statistical methods and with human annotation; filtering and cleaning monolingual and bilingual dictionaries to make them consistent; and computing grammatical transfer rules. Although the monolingual and bilingual dictionaries require the same entries, the function of each one is different. The monolingual dictionary contains morphological information and the bilingual dictionary contains the translation entry itself.

This first track of development has taken place in over the course of five months, which contrasts with the long time required to develop classical RBMT systems. The key point here is that our system has been developed using a hybrid approach and that, although the system is capable of achieving state-of-the-art translations, it is still under construction. The last version of the system is available for download at the Apertium site[1].

### 2.2 Bilingual dictionary

The bilingual dictionary was computed following two methodologies or procedures.

The first one is manual by using the Yellow Bridge resource[2]. This web is, as mentioned by the authors, the premier guide to Chinese language and culture for English speakers. They provide comprehensive tools for learning the Chinese language. Although there are many Chinese-related websites, this one is well-organized and complete. For Chinese, they provide a list of words classified following grammatical categories, including: adjectives, adverbs, conjunctions, interjections, measure words, nouns, numerals, onomatopoeia, particles, prefixes, prepositions, pronouns, question words, suffixes, time words and different types of verbs. For each category, each word has its corresponding translation into English. Then, this dictionary was used to feed the dictionary. But to double-check the translations provided, each word was translated using another on-line dictionary[3] and Google Translate. This procedure allowed to add several hundreds of numerals, conjunctions, adverbs, pronouns, determinants, adjectives, 3,000 nouns and 2,000 verbs.

The second procedure is statistical-based. The parallel corpus of the United Nations (UN) (Rafalovitch and Dale, 2009) was aligned at the

[1] http://sourceforge.net/projects/

[2] http://www.yellowbridge.com/chinese/chinese-parts-of-speech.php

[3] http://www.chinese-tools.com/

level of word by using the standard GIZA++ (Och and Ney, 2003) software. Alignment was performed from source to target and target to source. Symmetrization was done using intersection because it provides the most reliable links. Then, we extracted phrases of length one, which means that we extracted translations from word-to-word. This dictionary was manually filtered to eliminate incorrect entries. This procedure allowed to add around 3,500 words in the dictionaries. Our dictionary has around 9,000 words.

### 2.3 Chinese monolingual dictionary

The Chinese monolingual dictionary was extracted from the source part of the bilingual dictionary. Additionally, it was filtered with regular expressions to avoid repeated entries.

Regarding the morphological analysis, Chinese is an isolating language, which in brief means that words (or symbols) cannot be segmented in submorphemes. In this sense, no morphological analysis is required. However, the main challenge of Chinese is that most of the time symbols appear concatenated and sentences are not segmented into words as it is most common in other languages. Therefore, Chinese requires to be segmented. We used the ZhSeg (Dyer, 2013) programmed in C++. We evaluated the performance of this segmenter in comparison to the Left to Right Longest Match (LRLM), which is the parsing strategy used by Apertium in analysis mode. This procedure read tokens from left to right, matching the longest sequence that is in the dictionary (like "greedy" matching of regular expressions). Both ZhSeg and LRLM were compared using an in-house segmented test set of 456 words as a reference. The Word Error Rate (WER) measure for the ZhSeg was 16.56% and 16.89% for LRLM. Given that results were comparable, we decided to use the Apertium LRLM strategy.

It is mandatory that the monolingual and the bilingual dictionary are coherent, which means that they have to have the same entries. Both dictionaries were cleaned up with different regular expressions. Therefore, we have to ensure that there are not situations like there is a word in the monolingual dictionary, which is not in the bilingual dictionary and the other way round. In order to check out this, we used testvoc. As mentioned in the Apertium documentation [4], a testvoc is literally a test of vocabulary. At the most basic level, it just expands the monolingual dictionary, and runs each possibly analyzed lexical form through all the translation stages to see that for each possible input, a sensible translation in the target language is generated. This tool was used to clean up dictionaries.

[4] http://wiki.apertium.org/wiki/Testvoc

### 2.4 Spanish generation

This part of the translator was taken from the repository of Apertium given that is has been developed during years. Some previous publications that explain Spanish generation can by found in (Armentano-Oller et al., 2006; Corbí-Bellot et al., 2005). Basically, it consists of the three modules of Apertium: morphological generator that delivers a surface (inflected) form for each transferred word. This is done using the generation dictionary, which for each lemma and part-of-speech tag is able to generate the final form. Then, the post-generator that performs orthographic operations such as contractions (e.g. *de el* and *del*).

### 2.5 Transfer-rules

Grammatical transfer-rules were extracted following a manual procedure, which consisted in performing a translation of a source text and contrasting the output translation, the source and the reference. From this observation, manual patterns were extracted in order to design a rule that could cover the necessary modifications to be done. Following this procedure, there were 28 rules extracted intrasyntagms, which modify inside a syntagm, and 34 intersyntagms, which modify among different sytnagms.

As follows we show an example of rule extracted intrasyntagm.

```
< rule comment = RULE : adj nom >
 < pattern >
  < pattern − itemn = adj/ >
  < pattern − itemn = nom/ >
 < /pattern >
 < action >
 < call − macron = f − concord2 >
  < with − parampos = 2/ >
  < with − parampos = 1/ >
 < /call − macro >
 < out >
  < chunkname = j_ncase = caseFirstWord >
   < tags >
    < tag >< lit − tagv = SN/ >< /tag >
    < tag >< clip pos = 2side = tlpart = gen/ >< /tag >
    < tag >< clip pos = 2side = tlpart = nbr/ >< /tag >
    < tag >< lit − tagv = p3/ >< /tag >
   < /tags >
  < lu >
   < clip pos = 2side = tlpart = whole/ >
  < /lu >
  < b pos = 1/ >
   < lu >
    < clip pos = 1side = tlpart = lem/ >
```

```
    < clip pos = 1side = tlpart = a_adj/ >
    < clip pos = 1side = tlpart = gen/ >
    < clip pos = 1side = tlpart = nbr/ >
   < /lu >
  < /chunk >
 < /out >
 < /action >
< /rule >
```

This rule reorders *adjective* + *noun* into *noun* + *adjective*. Moreover, this rule ensures that the number and gender of the noun and the adjective agree.

## 3 Evaluation framework

This section reports the evaluation framework we have used to analyze the quality of the Chinese-to-Spanish RBMT described.

| Dataset | Domain | Words | Coverage |
|---|---|---|---|
| Dev | News | 1,651 | 88.7 |
| Test | UN | 35,914 | 83.8 |
| | In-house | 10,361 | 82.8 |

Table 1: Coverage results.

We can evaluate the rule-based MT systems in terms of coverage. We are using texts from different domains to perform the evaluation. Domains include news (extracted from the web[5,6]) for checking the evolution of the rule-based system; a subcorpus of UN (Rafalovitch and Dale, 2009); and an in-house developed small corpus in the transportation and hospitality domains. To do the evaluation of coverage we do not need a reference of translation. Table 1 shows the coverage results of our system.

This rule-based MT approach can be the baseline system towards a hybrid architecture. Inspired in previous promising works (España-Bonet et al., 2011), we have identified some ways of building a hybrid architecture given a rule-based MT system and available parallel and monolingual corpus:

- Starting with the core of a rule-based system, there is the necessity of extracting transfer-rules from parallel corpus and offering a translation probability to each one. This would allow to building rule-based MT systems by a monolingual human linguist. At the moment, rule-based MT systems have to be developed by bilingual native linguists or at least people who are proficient in the source and target language.

- In order to help rule-based MT systems be more fluent and natural, it would be nice to integrate a language model in the generation step. The language model could be n-gram-based, syntax-based or trained on neural-based. In each case, a different decoding would be required to be integrated in the system.

- Additional feature functions as the popular lexical ones or others that introduce source context information can be used together with the above language model.

## 4 Conclusions and further work

This paper has described the construction of the first Chinese-to-Spanish open-source RBMT system;. Particularly, the human knowledge has been used for providing exhaustive monolingual and bilingual dictionaries as well as for defining grammatical transfer rules. The statistical knowledge has complemented the creation of dictionaries. Therefore, we have shown effective techniques of building dictionaries using hybrid techniques. The new RBMT system has shown a high coverage in different domains.

As future work, the RBMT has to be improved mainly with new dictionary entries and more complex transfer rules. Both enhancements can be done combining human and statistical knowledge.

## 5 Acknowledgements

This work has been partially supported by the Google Summer of Code and the Seventh Framework Program of the European Commission through the International Outgoing Fellowship Marie Curie Action (IMTraP-2011-29951). Authors want to thank Apertium experts that believed in this project and helped a lot during the development, specially Francis Tyers, Víctor Sánchez-Cartagena, Filip Petkovsky, Gema Ramírez and Mikel Forcada.

[5]http://politics.people.com.cn/n/2013/0709/c1001-22134594.html

[6]http://finance.people.com.cn/n/2013/0722/c1004-22275982.html

## References


C. Armentano-Oller, R. C. Carrasco, A. M. Corb-Bellot, M. L. Forcada, M. Ginestí-Rosell, S. Ortiz-Rojas, J. A. Pérez-Ortiz, G. Ramírez-Sánchez, F. Sánchez-Martínez, and M. A. Scalco. 2006. Open-source Portuguese-Spanish machine translation. In R. Vieira, P. Quaresma, M.d.G.V. Nunes, N.J. Mamede, C. Oliveira, and M.C. Dias, editors, *Computational Processing of the Portuguese Language, Proc. of the 7th International Workshop on Computational Processing of Written and Spoken Portuguese, PROPOR*, volume 3960 of *Lecture Notes in Computer Science*, pages 50–59. Springer-Verlag, May.

A. M. Corbí-Bellot, M. L. Forcada, S. Ortiz-Rojas, J. A. Pérez-Ortiz, G. Ramírez-Sánchez, F. Sánchez-Martínez, I. Alegria, A. Mayor, and K. Sarasola. 2005. An open-source shallow-transfer machine translation engine for the romance languages of spain. In *Proceedings of the Tenth Conference of the European Association for Machine Translation*, pages 79–86, May.

J. P. Martínez Cortés, J. O'Regan, and F. M. Tyers. 2012. Free/open source shallow-transfer based machine translation for spanish and aragonese. In *LREC*, pages 2153–2157.

M. R. Costa-Jussà, M. Farrús, J. B. Mariño, and J. A. R. Fonollosa. 2012a. Study and comparison of rule-based and statistical catalan-spanish machine translation systems. *Computing and Informatics*, 31(2):245–270.

M. R. Costa-jussà, C. A. Henríquez Q, and R. E. Banchs. 2012b. Evaluating indirect strategies for Chinese-Spanish statistical machine translation. *J. Artif. Int. Res.*, 45(1):761–780.

C. Dyer. 2013. http://code.google.com/p/zhseg/.

C. España-Bonet, G. Labaka, A. Díaz de Ilarraza, L. Màrquez, and K. Sarasola. 2011. Hybrid machine translation guided by a rule-based system. In *Proc of the 13th Machine Translation Summit*, pages 554–561, Xiamen, China, sep.

M. L. Forcada, M. Ginestí-Rosell, J. Nordfalk, J. O'Regan, S. Ortiz-Rojas, J. A. Pérez-Ortiz, F. Sánchez-Martínez, G. Ramírez-Sánchez, and F. M. Tyers. 2011. Apertium: a free/open-source platform for rule-based machine translation. *Machine Translation*, 25(2):127–144.

W. J. Hutchins and L. Sommers. 1992. An introduction to machine translation. *Academic Press*, 362.

F.J. Och and H. Ney. 2003. A systematic comparison of various statistical alignment models. *Computational Linguistics*, 29(1):19–51, March.

A. Rafalovitch and R. Dale. 2009. United Nations General Assembly Resolutions: A Six-Language Parallel Corpus. In *Proc. of the MT Summit XII*, pages 292–299, Ottawa.

Y. Zhang, N. Wu, and M. Yip. 2006. Lexical ambiguity resolution in chinese sentence processing. *Handbook of East Asian Psycholinguistics*, 1:268–278.

# Extracting Multiword Translations from Aligned Comparable Documents

Reinhard Rapp
Aix-Marseille Université, Laboratoire d'Informatique Fondamentale
F-13288 Marseille, France
reinhardrapp@gmx.de

Serge Sharoff
University of Leeds
Centre for Translation Studies
Leeds, LS2 9JT, UK
S.Sharoff@leeds.ac.uk

## Abstract

Most previous attempts to identify translations of multiword expressions using comparable corpora relied on dictionaries of single words. The translation of a multiword was then constructed from the translations of its components. In contrast, in this work we try to determine the translation of a multiword unit by analyzing its contextual behaviour in aligned comparable documents, thereby not presupposing any given dictionary. Whereas with this method translation results for single words are rather good, the results for multiword units are considerably worse. This is an indication that the type of multiword expressions considered here is too infrequent to provide a sufficient amount of contextual information. Thus indirectly it is confirmed that it should make sense to look at the contextual behaviour of the components of a multiword expression individually, and to combine the results.

## 1 Introduction

The task of identifying word translations from comparable text has received considerable attention. Some early papers include Fung (1995) and Rapp (1995). Fung (1995) utilized a context heterogeneity measure, thereby assuming that words with productive context in one language translate to words with productive context in another language, and words with rigid context translate into words with rigid context. In contrast, the underlying assumption in Rapp (1995) was that words which are translations of each other show similar co-occurrence patterns across languages. This assumption is effectively an extension of Harris' (1954) distributional hypotheses to the multilingual case.

This work was further elaborated in some by now classical papers, such as Fung & Yee (1998) and Rapp (1999). Based on these papers, the standard approach is to start from a dictionary of seed words, and to assume that the words occurring in the context of a source language word have similar meanings as the words occurring in the context of its target language translation.

There have been suggestions to eliminate the need for the seed dictionary. However, most attempts, such as Rapp (1995), Diab & Finch (2000) and Haghighi et al. (2008) did not work to an extent that the results would be useful for practical purposes. Only recently a more promising approach has been investigated: Schafer & Yarowsky (2002), Hassan & Mihalcea (2009), Prochasson & Fung (2011) and Rapp et al. (2012) look at aligned comparable documents and deal with them in analogy to the treatment of aligned parallel sentences, i.e. effectively doing a word alignment in a very noisy environment. This approach has been rather successful and it was possible to improve on previous results. This is therefore the approach which we will pursue in the current paper.

However, in contrast to the above mentioned papers the focus of our work is on multiword expressions, and we will compare the performance of our algorithm when applied to multiword expressions and when applied to single words.

There has been some previous work on identifying the translations of multiword units using comparable corpora, such as Robitaille et al. (2006), Babych et al. (2007), Daille & Morin (2012); Delpech et al. (2012). However, none of this work utilizes aligned comparable documents, and the underlying assumption is that the translation of a multiword unit can be determined by looking at its components individually, and by merging the results.

In contrast, we try to explore whether the translation of a multiword unit can be determined solely by looking at its contextual behavior, i.e. whether it is possible to also apply the standard approach as successfully used for single words. The underlying fundamental question is whether the meaning of a multiword unit is determined by the contextual behavior of the full unit, or by the contextual behavior of its components (or by a mix of both). But multiword expressions are of complex nature, as expressed e.g. by Moon (1998): "there is no unified phenomenon to describe but rather a complex of features that interact in various, often untidy, ways and represent a broad continuum between non-compositional (or idiomatic) and compositional groups of words." The current paper is an attempt to systematically approach one aspect of this complexity.

## 2 Approach

Our approach is based on the usual assumption that there is a correlation between the patterns of word-co-occurrence across languages. However, instead of presupposing a bilingual dictionary it only requires pre-aligned comparable documents, i.e. small or medium sized documents aligned across languages which are known to deal with similar topics. This could be, for example, newspaper articles, scientific papers, contributions to discussion groups, or encyclopaedic articles. As Wikipedia is a large resource and readily available for many languages, we decided to base our study on this encyclopaedia. The Wikipedias have the so-called interlanguage links which are manually inserted by the authors and connect articles referring to the same headword in different languages.

Given that each Wikipedia community contributes in its own language, only occasionally an article connected in this way will be an exact translation of a foreign language article, and in most cases the contents will be rather different. On the positive side, the link structure of the interlanguage links tends to be quite dense. For example, of the 1,114,696 German Wikipedia articles, 603,437 have a link to the corresponding English Wikipedia article.

### 2.1 Pre-processing and MWE extraction

We used the same versions of Wikipedia as in Rapp et al. (2012) and used the same processing. After download, each Wikipedia was minimally processed to extract the plain text contents of the articles. In this process all templates, e.g. 'infoboxes', as well as tables were removed, and we kept only the webpages with more than 500 characters of running text (including white space). Linguistic processing steps included tokenisation, tagging and lemmatisation using the default UTF-8 versions of the respective TreeTagger resources (Schmid, 1994).

From the pre-processed English and German Wikipedia, we extracted the multiword expressions using two simple principles, a *negative POS filter* and a *containment filter*. The negative POS filter operates in a rule-based fashion on the complete list of n-grams by removing the unlikely candidates according to a set of constraints, such as the presence of determiners or prepositions at the edges of expressions, see a similar method used by (Justeson & Katz, 1995). With some further extensions this was also used to produce the multiword lists for the dictionary of translation equivalents (Babych et al., 2007).

We did not use positive shallow filters. These would need to capture the relatively complex structure of the noun, verb and prepositional phrases, while avoiding noise. This can often lead to a lack of recall when more complex constructions cannot be captured. In contrast, negative shallow filters simply avoid obvious noise, while passing other multiword expressions (MWEs) through, which are very often legitimate syntactic constructions in a language in question. For example, the following English filters[1] rejected personal pronouns (PP) and conjunctions (CC) at the edges of expressions (using the Penn Treebank tagset as implemented by Treetagger):

```
^[^ ]+~~PP |~~PP$
^[^ ]+~~CC |~~CC$
```

Similarly, any MWE candidates including proper nouns (NP) and numerals (CD) were discarded:

```
~~NP
~~CD
```

In the end, this helps in improving the recall rate while using a relatively small number of patterns: 18 patterns were used for English, 11 for German.

The containment filter further rejects MWEs by removing those that regularly occur as a part of a longer acceptable MWE. For example, *graphical user* is an acceptable expression passing through the POS filter, but it is rejected by the containment filter since the overwhelming majority of its uses are in the containing MWE *graphical user interface* (1507 vs 1304 uses in Wikipedia, since MWEs are still possible, e.g., *graphical user environment*).

[1] We use here the standard notation for regular expressions as implemented in Perl (Friedl, 2002). For example, '^' means 'beginning of line' and '$' means 'end of line'.

| English keyterms for 'Airbus 320 family' | | |
|---|---|---|
| *Score* | *f* | *Keyterm* |
| 34.88 | 4 | final_JJ assembly_NN |
| 31.22 | 3 | firm_NN order_NN |
| 30.73 | 3 | series_NN aircraft_NN |
| 29.07 | 4 | flight_NN control_NN |
| 27.38 | 3 | wing_NN area_NN |
| 23.26 | 3 | final_JJ approach_NN |
| 22.19 | 2 | lose_VV life_NN |
| 20.63 | 6 | passenger_NN and_CC crew_NN |
| 17.54 | 2 | first_JJ derivative_NN |
| 17.34 | 2 | fly-by-wire_NN flight_NN control_NN |
| 16.63 | 3 | flight_NN deck_NN |
| 16.41 | 2 | crew_NN die_VV |
| 15.08 | 2 | pilot_NN error_NN |
| 14.98 | 2 | passenger_NN capacity_NN |
| 14.38 | 2 | turbofan_NN engine_NN |
| 14.03 | 2 | development_NN cost_NN |
| 12.30 | 2 | maiden_JJ flight_NN |
| 11.54 | 2 | direct_JJ competition_NN |
| 10.75 | 2 | overall_JJ length_NN |
| 10.39 | 2 | overrun_VV the_DT runway_NN |
| 9.54 | 2 | flight_NN control_NN system_NN |
| 9.31 | 2 | fuel_NN consumption_NN |
| 8.63 | 2 | roll_VV out_RP |
| 7.86 | 3 | crew_NN member_NN |
| 7.54 | 2 | crew_NN on_IN board_NN |
| 7.33 | 2 | bad_JJ weather_NN |
| 6.63 | 2 | landing_NN gear_NN |

| German keyterms for 'Airbus-A320-Familie' | | |
|---|---|---|
| *Score* | *f* | *Keyterm* |
| 155.25 | 20 | Triebwerk |
| 62.88 | 4 | Fly-by-Wire-System |
| 59.76 | 8 | Erstflug |
| 57.67 | 8 | Absturz |
| 43.79 | 4 | Endmontage |
| 43.70 | 4 | Hauptfahrwerk |
| 41.77 | 4 | Tragflügel |
| 36.52 | 8 | Unfall |
| 35.90 | 6 | Unglück |
| 33.25 | 3 | Abfluggewicht |
| 33.10 | 5 | Auslieferung |
| 30.01 | 3 | Treibstoffverbrauch |
| 29.00 | 2 | Triebwerkstyp |
| 28.51 | 2 | Zwillingsreifen |
| 18.20 | 2 | Absturz_NN verursachen_VV |
| 16.28 | 3 | Passagier_NN Platz_NN |
| 16.23 | 2 | Triebwerk_NN antreiben_VV |
| 13.41 | 2 | Steuerung_NN d_AR Flugzeug_NN |
| 12.52 | 2 | Absturz_NN führen_VV |
| 11.68 | 2 | Rumpf_NN befinden_VV |
| 8.59 | 2 | Insasse_NN ums_AP Leben_NN |
| 8.55 | 2 | Zeitpunkt_NN d_AR Unglück_NN |

Table 1. English and German keyterms for 'Airbus 320 family' (lists truncated). Score = log-likelihood score; f = occurrence frequency of keyterm; NN = noun; VV = verb; AR = article; AP = article+preposition; JJ = adjective; CC = conjunction; RP = preposition.

## 2.2 Keyterm extraction

As the aligned English and German Wikipedia documents are typically not translations of each other, we cannot apply the usual procedures and tools as available for parallel texts (e.g. the Gale & Church sentence aligner and the Giza++ word alignment tool). Instead we conduct a two step procedure:

1. We first extract salient terms (single word or multiword) from each of the documents.
2. We then align these terms across languages using an approach inspired by a connectionist (Rumelhart & McClelland, 1987) Winner-Takes-It-All Network. The respective algorithm is called WINTIAN and is described in Rapp et al. (2012) and in Rapp (1996).

For term extraction, the occurrence frequency of a term in a particular document is compared to its average occurrence frequency in all Wikipedia documents, whereby a high discrepancy indicates a strong keyness. Following Rayson & Garside (2000), we use the log-likelihood score to measure keyness, since it has been shown to be robust to small numbers of instances. This robustness is important as many Wikipedia articles are rather short.

This procedure leads to multiword keyterms as exemplified in Table 1 for the Wikipedia entry *Airbus A320 family*. Because of compounding in German, many single-word German expressions are translated into multiword expressions in English. So we chose to include single-word expressions into the German candidate list for alignment with English multiwords.

One of the problems in obtaining multiword keyterms from the Wikipedia articles is relative data sparseness. Usually, the frequency of an individual multiword expression within a Wikipedia article is between 2 and 4. Therefore we had to use a less conservative threshold of 6.63 (1% significance level) rather than the more standard 15.13 (0.01% significance level) for the log-likelihood score (see Rayson & Garside, 2000, and http://ucrel. lancs.ac.uk/llwizard.html).

## 2.3 Term alignment

The WINTIAN algorithm is used for establishing term alignments across languages. As a more detailed technical description is given in Rapp et al. (2012) and in Rapp (1996), we only briefly describe this algorithm here, thereby focusing on the neural network analogy. The algorithm can be considered as an artificial neural network where the nodes are all English and German terms occurring in the keyterm lists. Each English term has connections to all German terms. The connections are all initialized with values of one when the algorithm is started, but will serve as a measure of the translation probabilities after the completion of the algorithm. One after the other, the network is fed with the pairs of corresponding keyterm lists. Each German term activates the corresponding German node with an activity of one. This activity is then propagated to all English terms occurring in the corresponding list of keyterms. The distribution of the activity is not equal, but in proportion to the connecting weights. This unequal distribution has no effect at the beginning when all weights are one, but later on leads to rapid activity increases for pairs of terms which often occur in corresponding keyterm lists. The assumption is that these are translations of each other. Using Hebbian learning (Rumelhart & McClelland, 1987) the activity changes are stored in the connections. We use a heuristic to avoid the effect that frequent keyterms dominate the network: When more than 50 of the connections to a particular English node have weights higher than one, the weakest 20 of them are reset to one. This way only translations which are frequently confirmed can build up high weights.

It turned out that the algorithm shows a robust behaviour in practice, which is important as the corresponding keyterm lists tend to be very noisy and, especially for multiword expressions, in many cases may contain hardly any terms that are actually translations of each other. Reasons are that corresponding Wikipedia articles are often written from different perspectives, that the variation in length can be considerable across languages, and that multiword expressions tend to show more variability with regard to their translations than single words.

## 3 Results and evaluation

### 3.1 Results for single words

In this subsection we report on our previous results for single words (Rapp et al., 2012) as these serve as a baseline for our new results concerning multiword units.

The WINTIAN algorithm requires as input vocabularies of the source and the target language. For both English and German, we constructed these as follows: Based on the keyword lists for the respective Wikipedia, we counted the number of occurrences of each keyword, and then applied a threshold of five, i.e. all keywords with a lower frequency were eliminated. The reasoning behind this is that rare keywords are of not much use due to data sparseness. This resulted in a vocabulary size of 133,806 for English, and of 144,251 for German.

Using the WINTIAN algorithm, the English translations for all 144,251 words occurring in the German vocabulary were computed. Table 2 shows the results for the German word *Straße* (which means *street*).

For a quantitative evaluation we used the ML1000 test set comprising 1000 English-German translations (see Rapp et al., 2012). We verified in how many cases our algorithm had assigned the expected translation (as provided by the gold standard) the top rank among all 133,806 translation candidates. (Candidates are all words occurring in the English vocabulary.) This was the case for 381 of the 1000 items, which gives us an accuracy of 38.1%. Let us mention that this result refers to exact matches with the word equations in the gold standard. As in reality due to word ambiguity other translations might also be acceptable (e.g. for *Straße* not only *street* but also *road* would be acceptable), these figures are conservative and can be seen as a lower bound of the actual performance.

| GIVEN GERMAN WORD | *Straße* | |
|---|---|---|
| EXPECTED TRANSLATION | *street* | |
| | LL-SCORE | TRANSLATION |
| 1 | 215.3 | road |
| 2 | 148.2 | street |
| 3 | 66.0 | traffic |
| 4 | 46.0 | Road |
| 5 | 42.6 | route |
| 6 | 34.6 | building |

Table 2. Computed translations for *Straße*.

### 3.2 Results for multiword expressions

In analogy to the procedure for single words, for the WINTIAN algorithm we also needed to define English and German vocabularies of multiword terms. For English, we selected all multiword terms which occurred at least three times in the lists of English key terms, and for German those which occurred at least four times in the lists of German key terms. This resulted in similar sized vocabularies of 114,796 terms for English, and 131,170 for German. Note that the threshold for German had to be selected higher not because German has more inflectional variants (which does not matter as we are working with lemmatized data), but because – other than the English – the German vocabulary also includes unigrams. The reason for this is that German is highly compositional, so that English multiword units are often translated by German unigrams.

Using the WINTIAN algorithm, the English translations for all 131,170 words occurring in the German multiword vocabulary were computed, and in another run the German translations for all 114,796 English words. Table 3 shows some sample results.

For a quantitative evaluation, we did not have a gold standard at hand. As multiword expressions show a high degree of variability with regard to their translations, so that it is hard to come up with all possibilities, we first decided not to construct a gold standard, but instead did a manual evaluation. For this purpose, we randomly selected 100 of the German multiword expressions with an occurrence frequency above nine, and verified their computed translations (i.e. the top ranked item for each) manually. We distinguished three categories: 1) Acceptable translation; 2) Associatively related to an acceptable translation; 3) Unrelated to an acceptable translation.

| | *English → German* | |
|---|---|---|
| | husband_NN and_CC wife_NN | |
| *Rank* | *Aktivity* | *Translation* |
| 1 | 2.98 | Eheleute |
| 2 | 1.09 | Voraussetzung |
| 3 | 1.08 | Kirchenrecht |
| 4 | 0.76 | Trennung |
| 5 | 0.35 | Mann |
| 6 | 0.24 | Kirche |
| 7 | 0.08 | Mischehe |
| 8 | 0.08 | Diakon |

| | *German → English* | |
|---|---|---|
| | Eheleute | |
| *Rank* | *Aktivity* | *Translation* |
| 1 | 3.01 | husband_NN_and_CC_wife_NN |
| 2 | 1.26 | married_JJ_couple_NN |
| 3 | 1.02 | civil_JJ_law_NN |
| 4 | 1.02 | equitable_JJ_distribution_NN |
| 5 | 1.02 | community_NN_property_NN |
| 6 | 0.52 | law_NN_jurisdiction_NN |
| 7 | 0.05 | racing_NN_history_NN |
| 8 | 0.05 | great_JJ_female_JJ |

Table 3. Sample results for translation directions EN → DE and DE → EN.

We also did the same computation for the reverse language direction, i.e. for English to German. The results are listed in Table 4. These results indicate that our procedure, although currently state of the art for single words, does not work well for multiword units. We investigated the data and located the following problems:

- The problem of data sparseness is, on average, considerably more severe for multiword expressions than it is for single words.
- Although the English and the German vocabulary each contain more than 100,000 items, their overlap is still limited. The reason is that the number of possible multiword units is very high, far higher than the number of words in a language.
- We considered only multiword units up to length three, but in some cases this may not suffice for an acceptable translation.
- In the aligned keyterm lists, only rarely correct translations of the source language terms occur. Apparently the reason is the high variability of multiword translations.

Hereby he last point seems to have a particularly severe negative effect on translation quality. However, all of these findings are of fundamental nature and contribute to the insight that at least for our set of multiword expressions compositionality seems to be more important than contextuality.

| German → English | | |
|---|---|---|
| *Judgment* | *Number* | *Example taken from actual data* |
| Acceptable | 5 | Jugendherberge → youth_NN hostel_NN |
| Association | 38 | Maischegärung → oak_NN barrel_NN |
| Unacceptable | 57 | Stachelbeere → horror_NN film_NN |

| English → German | | |
|---|---|---|
| *Judgment* | *Number* | *Example taken from actual data* |
| Acceptable | 6 | amino_NN acid_NN → Aminosäure |
| Association | 52 | iron_NN mine_NN → Eisenerz |
| Unacceptable | 42 | kill_VV more_JJ → Weltmeistertitel_NN im_AP Schwergewicht_NN |

Table 4. Quantitative results involving MWEs.

### 3.3 Large scale evaluation

As a manual evaluation like the one described above is time consuming and subjective, we thought about how we could efficiently come up with a gold standard for multiword expressions with the aim of conducting a large scale automatic evaluation. We had the idea to determine the correspondences between our English and German MWEs via translation information as extracted from a word-aligned parallel corpus.

Such data we had readily at hand from a previous project called COMTRANS. During this project we had constructed a large bilingual dictionary of bigrams, i.e. of pairs of adjacent words in the source language. For constructing the dictionary, we word-aligned the English and German parts of the Europarl corpus. For this purpose, using Moses default settings, we combined two symmetric runs of Giza++, which considerably improves alignment quality. Then we determined and extracted for each English bigram the German word or word sequence which had been used for its translation. Discontinuities of one or several word positions were allowed and were indicated by the wildcard '*'. As the above method for word alignment produces many unjustified empty assignments (i.e. assignments where a source language word pair is erroneously assumed to have no equivalent in the target language sentence), so that the majority of these is incorrect, all empty assignments were removed from the dictionary.

In the dictionary, for each source language word pair its absolute frequency and the absolute and relative frequencies of its translation(s) are given. To filter out spurious assignments, thresholds of 2 for the absolute and 10% for the relative frequency of a translation were used. The resulting dictionary is available online.[2] Table 5 shows a small extract of the altogether 371,590 dictionary entries. Alternatively, we could have started from a Moses phrase table, but it was easier for us to use our own data.

Although the quality of our bigram dictionary seems reasonably good, it contains a lot of items which are not really interesting multiword expressions (e.g. arbitrary word sequences such as *credible if* or the discontinuous word sequences on the target language side). For this reason we filtered the dictionary using the lists of Wikipedia-derived multiword expressions as described in section 2.1. These contained 418,627 items for English and 1,212,341 candidate items for German (the latter included unigram compounds). That is, in the dictionary those items were removed where either the English side did not match any of the English MWEs, or where the German side did not match any of the German candidates.

This intersection resulted in a reduction of our bigram dictionary from 371,590 items to 137,701 items. Table 6 shows the results after filtering the items listed in Table 5. Note that occasionally reasonable MWEs are eliminated if they happen not to occur in Wikipedia, or if the algorithm for extracting the MWEs does not identify them.

The reduced dictionary we considered as an appropriate gold standard for the automatic evaluation of our system.

| ENGLISH BIGRAM | GERMAN TRANSLATION |
|---|---|
| credible if | dann glaubwürdig * wenn |
| credible if | glaubhaft * wenn |
| credible if | glaubwürdig * wenn |
| credible in | in * Glaubwürdigkeit |
| credible in | in * glaubwürdig |
| credible investigation | glaubwürdige Untersuchung |
| credible labelling | glaubwürdige Kennzeichnung |
| credible manner | glaubwürdig |
| credible military | glaubwürdige militärische |
| credible military | glaubwürdigen militärischen |
| credible only | nur dann glaubwürdig |
| credible partner | glaubwürdiger Partner |
| credible policy | Politik * glaubwürdig |
| credible policy | glaubwürdige Politik |
| credible reports | glaubwürdige Berichte |
| credible response | glaubwürdige Antwort |
| credible solution | glaubwürdige Lösung |
| credible system | glaubwürdiges System |
| credible threat | glaubhafte Androhung |
| credible to | für * glaubwürdig |
| credible to | glaubwürdig |

Table 5. Extract from the COMTRANS bigram dictionary.

| ENGLISH BIGRAM | GERMAN TRANSLATION |
|---|---|
| credible investigation | glaubwürdige Untersuchung |
| credible only | nur dann glaubwürdig |
| credible policy | glaubwürdige Politik |
| credible response | glaubwürdige Antwort |
| credible solution | glaubwürdige Lösung |
| credible system | glaubwürdiges System |
| credible threat | glaubhafte Androhung |
| credible to | glaubwürdig |

Table 6. Extract from the bigram dictionary after filtering.

[2] http://www.ftsk.uni-mainz.de/user/rapp/comtrans/
There click on "Dictionaries of word pairs" and then download "English - German".

As in section 3.2, the next step was to apply the keyword extraction algorithm to the English and the German Wikipedia documents. Hereby only terms occurring in the gold standard dictionary were taken into account. But it turned out that, when using the same log-likelihood threshold as in section 3.2, only few keyterms were assigned: on average less than one per document. This had already been a problem in 3.2, but it was now considerably more severe as this time the MWE lists had been filtered, and as the filtering had been on the basis of another type of corpus (Europarl rather than Wikipedia).

This is why, after some preliminary experiments with various thresholds, we finally decided to disable the log-likelihood threshold. Instead, on the English side, all keyterms from the gold standard were used if they occurred at least once in the respective Wikipedia document. On the German side, as here we had many unigram compounds which tend to be more stable and therefore more repetitive than MWEs, we used the keyterms if the occurred at least twice. This way for most documents we obtained at least a few keyterms.

When running the WINTIAN algorithm on the parallel keyword lists, in some cases reasonable results were obtained. For example, for the direction English to German, the system translates *information society* with *Informationsgesellschaft*, and *education policy* with *Bildungspolitik*. As WINTIAN is symmetric and can likewise produce a dictionary in the opposite direction, we also generated the results for German to English. Here, among the good examples, are *Telekommunikationsmarkt*, which is translated as *telecommunications market*, and *Werbekampagne*, which is translated as *advertising campaign*. However, these are selected examples showing that the algorithm works in principle.

Of more interest is the quantitative evaluation which is based on thousands of test words and uses the gold standard dictionary. For English to German we obtained an accuracy of 0.77% if only the top ranked word is taken into account, i.e. if this word matches the expected translation. This improves to 1.6% if it suffices that the expected translation is ranked among the top ten words. The respective figures for German to English are 1.41% and 2.04%.

The finding that German to English performs better can be explained by the fact that other than English German is a highly inflectional language. That is, when generating translations it is more likely for German that an inflectional variant not matching the gold standard translation is ranked first, thus adversely affecting performance.

A question more difficult to answer is why the results based on the gold standard are considerably worse than the ones reported in section 3.2 which were based on human judgment. We see the following reasons:

- The evaluation in section 3.2 used only a small sample so might be not very reliable. Also, other than here, it considered only source language words with frequencies above nine.
- Unlike the candidate expressions, the gold standard data is not lemmatized on the target language side.
- The hard string matching used for the gold-standard-based evaluation does not allow for inflectional variants.
- The gold-standard-based evaluation used terms resulting from the intersection of term lists based on Wikipedia and Europarl. It is clear that this led to a reduction of average term frequency (if measured on the basis of Wikipedia), thus increasing the problem of data sparseness.
- As for the same reason the log-likelihood threshold had to be abandoned, on average less salient terms had to be used. This is likely to additionally reduce accuracy.
- For many terms the gold standard lists several possible translations. In the current implementation of the evaluation algorithm only one of them is counted as correct.[3] However, in the human evaluation any reasonable translation was accepted.
- Some reasonable MWE candidates extracted from Wikipedia are not present in the gold standard, for example *credible evidence*, *credible source*, and *credible witness* are not frequent enough in Europarl to be selected for alignment.

We should perhaps mention that it would be possible to come up with better looking accuracies by presenting results for selected subsets of the source language terms. For example, one could concentrate on terms with particularly good cov-

[3] This can be justified because an optimal algorithm should provide all possible translations of a term. If only some translations are provided, only partial credit should be given. But this is likely to average out over large numbers, so the simple version seems acceptable.

erage. Another possibility would be to consider MWEs consisting of nouns only. This we actually did by limiting source and target language vocabulary (of MWEs) to compound nouns. The results were as follows:

| | |
|---|---|
| English to German (top 1): | 1.81% |
| English to German (top 10): | 3.75% |
| German to English (top 1): | 2.03% |
| German to English (top 10): | 3.16% |

As can be seen, these results look somewhat better. But this is only for the reason that translating compound nouns appears to be a comparatively easier task on average.

## 4 Conclusions and future work

We have presented a method for identifying term translations using aligned comparable documents. Although it is based on a knowledge poor approach and does not presuppose a seed lexicon, it delivers competitive results for single words.

A disadvantage of our method is that it presupposes that the alignments of the comparable documents are known. On the other hand, there are methods for finding such alignments automatically not only in special cases such as Wikipedia and newspaper texts, but also in the case of unstructured texts (although these methods may require a seed lexicon).

Concerning the question from the introduction, namely whether the translation (and consequently also the meaning) of a multiword unit is determined compositionally or contextually, our answer is as follows: For the type of multiword units we were investigating, namely automatically extracted collocations, our results indicate that looking at their contextual behavior usually does not suffice. The reasons seem to be that their contextual behavior shows a high degree of variability, that their translations tend to be less salient than those of single words, and that the problem of data sparseness is considerably more severe.

It must be seen, however, that there are many types of multiword expressions, such as idioms, metaphorical expressions, named entities, fixed phrases, noun compounds, compound verbs, compound adjectives, and so on, so that our results are not automatically applicable to all of them. Therefore, in future work we intend to compare the behavior of different types of multiword expressions (e.g. multiword named entities and short phrases such as those used in phrase-based machine translations) and to quantify in how far their behavior is compositional or contextual.

## Acknowledgment

This research was supported by a Marie Curie Intra European Fellowship within the 7th European Community Framework Programme.

## References

Babych, B., Sharoff, S., Hartley, A., and Mudraya, O. (2007). Assisting Translators in Indirect Lexical Transfer. *Proceedings of the 45th Annual Meeting of the Association for Computational Linguistics ACL 2007*, Prague, Czech Republic.

Daille, B.; Morin, E. (2012). Revising the compositional method for terminology acquisition from comparable corpora. Proceedings of Coling 2012, Mumbai.

Delpech, E.; Daille, B.; Morin, E., Lemaire, C. (2012). Extraction of domain-specific bilingual lexicon from comparable corpora: compositional translation and ranking. Proceedings of Coling 2012, Mumbai.

Diab, M., Finch, S. (2000): A statistical wordlevel translation model for comparable corpora. In: *Proceedings of the Conference on Content-Based Multimedia Information Access* (RIAO).

Friedl, J. (2002). *Mastering Regular Expressions.* O'Reilly.

Fung, P. (1995). Compiling bilingual lexicon entries from a non-parallel English-Chinese corpus. In: *Proceedings of the Third Annual Workshop on Very Large Corpora*, Boston, Massachusetts. 173-183.

Fung, P.; Yee, L. Y. (1998). An IR approach for translating new words from nonparallel, comparable texts. *Proceedings of COLING/ACL 1998, Montreal, Canada.* 414-420.

Haghighi, A., Liang, P., Berg-Kirkpatrick, T., Klein, D. (2008): Learning bilingual lexicons from monolingual corpora. In: Proceedings of ACL-HLT 2008, Columbus, Ohio. 771-779.

Harris, Z.S. (1954). Distributional structure. *Word*, 10(23), 146–162.

Hassan, S., Mihalcea, R. (2009): Cross-lingual semantic relatedness using encyclopedic knowledge. In: *Proceedings of EMNLP*.

Justeson, J.S.; Katz, S.M. (1995). Techninal terminology: some linguistic properties and an algorithm for identification in text. *Natural Language Engineering*, 1(1): 9–27.

Moon, R.E. 1998. Fixed Expressions and Idioms in English: A Corpus-based Approach. Oxford: Clarendon Press.

Prochasson, E., Fung, P. (2011). Rare word translation extraction from aligned comparable documents. In: *Proceedings of ACL-HLT*. Portland .

Rapp, R. (1995). Identifying word translations in non-parallel texts. In: Proceedings *of the 33rd Annual Meeting of the ACL*. Cambridge, MA, 320-322.

Rapp, R. (1996). *Die Berechnung von Assoziationen*. Hildesheim: Olms.

Rapp, R. (1999). Automatic identification of word translations from unrelated English and German corpora. *Proceedings of the 37th Annual Meeting of the Association for Computational Linguistics, College Park, Maryland*. 519–526.

Rapp, R., Sharoff, S., Babych, B. (2012). Identifying word translations from comparable documents without a seed lexicon. In: Proceedings of the 8th Language Resources and Evaluation Conference, LREC 2012, Istanbul.

Rayson, P.; Garside, R. (2000). Comparing corpora using frequency profiling. *Proceedings of the Workshop on Comparing Corpora (WCC '00 ), Volume 9*, 1–6.

Robitaille, X., Sasaki, Y., Tonoike, M., Sato, S., Utsuro, T. (2006). Compiling French-Japanese terminologies from the web. In: Proceedings of the 11th Conference of EACL, Trento, Italy, 225-232.

Rumelhart, D.E.; McClelland, J.L. (1987). *Parallel Distributed Processing. Explorations in the Microstructure of Cognition. Volume 1: Foundations*. MIT Press.

Schafer, C., Yarowsky, D (2002).: Inducing translation lexicons via diverse similarity measures and bridge languages. In: *Proceedings of CoNLL*.

Schmid, H. (1994). Probabilistic part-of-speech tagging using decision trees. *International Conference on New Methods in Language Processing*, 44–49.

# How to overtake Google in MT quality - the Baltic case

**Andrejs Vasiljevs**

Tilde Company

Vienibas gatve 75a
LV1004 Riga
LATVIA
Andrejs@Tilde.lv

## Abstract

Motivation of the language technology company Tilde is to improve quality of machine translation for lesser resourced languages such as the languages of Baltic countries. Generic MT solutions like Google Translate perform poorly for these complex languages. To compensate the shortage of training data and to deal with rich morphology we are applying different approaches in combining statistical methods with linguistic rules. We will present the strategies applied and the results of various experiments. We will discuss application of the production systems that show significantly better translation quality comparing to the Google Translate. We will also outline how this work contributes to creation of the European infrastructure for automated translation.

# Hybrid Strategies for better products and shorter time-to-market

**Kurt Eberle**

Lingenio GmbH

Karlsruher Straße 10
69126 Heidelberg
Germany
k.eberle@lingenio.de

## Abstract

The main Lingenio MT products are based on rule-based architectures. In the presentation we show how knowledge from corpora is integrated into the systems using the language analysis- and translation-components in a bootstrapping approach. This relates to the bilingual dictionaries, but also to learning decisions concerning the selection of syntactic rules and semantic readings in parsing and semantic evaluation. These strategies contribute both to improve the quality of the systems and to shorten go-to-market of new products significantly. Also a number of attractive spin-off functions can be generated from them which, in addition, can be used for designing new types of products and as preparatory and postediting features in MT systems whose core is of type SMT.

# Author Index